Dick Tiger Inc.
UNDAUNTED

Dick Tiger Inc.
UNDAUNTED

Justina Ihetu

1603 Capitol Ave., Suite 310 Cheyenne, Wyoming USA 82001
1-888-980-6523 | admin@urlinkpublishing.com

URLink Print and Media is committed to excellence in the publishing industry.

Book design copyright © 2023 by URLink Print and Media. All rights reserved.

Published in the United States of America

Library of Congress Control Number: 2023905095
ISBN 978-1-68486-393-8 (Paperback)
ISBN 978-1-68486-395-2 (Digital)

13.03.23

In memory of my beloved parents, Abigail and Richard (Dick Tiger) Ihetu, for their indelible prints in the sands of time.

Introduction

Justina Ihetu has written a gratifying story about a courageous and important figure in the history of twentieth century Africa. Her father, Dick Tiger, was a lion in the ring, but a wise owl in his everyday life.

We experience his heroic story from the multiple perspectives of the village, the nation, and the expatriate community. The event that propels the tale is the first world championship fight that took place in Africa. We witness and live alongside the participants in this epic battle between Dick Tiger and Gene Fullmer. The clear winner in this great contest is, surely, the audience.

Steve Fagin, Professor,
Visual Arts Department,
University of California,
San Diego.

Indifference to history isn't just ignorant, it's rude.
It's a form of ingratitude.

Historian, David McCullough.

Acknowledgement

I owe a debt of gratitude to a host of people who helped me along the way with encouragements and the seed stories that have brought forth this production. I may not be able to mention all one by one, but be assured, you are greatly appreciated. A mention to my uncles, Eze Ezeabasirim and Ebere Ihejirika, for their invaluable support. Lolo Comfort Ihetu, thank you so much for the excitement and energy you brought to storytelling. It proved infectious!

A world of thanks to authors of books and articles about my father, especially to Mr. Adeyinka Makinde, for his conviction and impeccable research upon which I launched my own journey of discovery. To Mr. John Sheppard and his team at BoxRec, I hail you, for keeping boxings glorious past present, even as you spotlight latest talents in boxing. Thank you, Mr. Ron Lipton, who's seen it all in boxing, and continues to tell it all, about Dick Tiger, and other boxing greats.

Dr Chamberlain Diala (Chamba), my brother from another mother, I remain grateful to you for being an inspiration.

To my daughter, Alexis Onyinyechi, and my son, Daniel Chukwunonso, for allowing me the space and peace of mind to achieve this goal, I love you guys more.

I remain indebted to the memory of my late uncles, Pa Godwin Ihetu and Pa Gordy "Goldsmith" Uzoaru, for their counsel and for being my window into the past.

Preface

The great Dick Tiger, undisputed three-time world boxing champion, is also indisputably a major player in two very defining moments in Nigeria's history: one of a glorious nature, when he dueled with Gene Fullmer before his countrymen in the ancient city of Ibadan, Nigeria, and the other, of the inglorious civil war in Nigeria. In both circumstances, Dick Tiger evoked a sense of pride, courage, and hope.

Rooted in family, Dick Tiger was a loving husband and devoted father of eight. A journeyman boxer, he travelled from Nigerian boxing booths, to the slum gyms of Liverpool and Blackpool, and finally, to boxing glory. Family and country were everything to Dick Tiger. As he fought in the ring, he clung to a singular thought—to provide enough for family, and make his fledgling nation of Nigeria proud. This thought was utmost in his mind when he campaigned to bring a world championship match to Nigeria. His efforts paid off, and on August 10, 1963, the first ever world boxing championship event on African soil took place in the city of Ibadan, Nigeria.

Dick Tiger wore his heart on his sleeve and was never able to ignore a problem that caused people distress. Mr. Ted Brenner, of Madison Square Garden, put it aptly when he said, "The thing about Dick Tiger is that he has an honest heart and willing hands. If he gets beat, it's only because the other guy was a better fighter that night. He usually gives away height and weight and age. But he never gives away heart."

Coming from a humble background in the rustic backwoods of Eastern Nigeria, Dick Tiger's humble beginnings certainly gave no indication that he would become one of the greatest middleweight boxing champions of all time. Described as an aggressive counterpuncher with a powerful left hook, he would stalk his opponent like a tiger, to draw him into a fist battle and counter with extremely hard punches and blows to the body. That was his own special modus operandi in the roped ring.

He started boxing professionally in 1952, and a few years later, he moved to Britain to further his boxing career. Although pitted against only the toughest of contenders in the science of boxing, from each misstep and fall, Tiger bounced back and refined his skills to beat down the next opponent. For his fistic prowess and popularity, Queen Elizabeth II honored him with a medal as a member of the Order of the British Empire (MBE). He was twice honored by the Boxing Writers Association as Fighter of the Year in 1963 and 1966. No other boxer had been so honored in the sixties decade. As a result of Dick Tiger's achievements in and out of the boxing ring, I am able to partake in a glorious legacy of self-actualization and service. This realization has inspired me and given me a sense of direction and personal enhancement.

Change can come slowly sometimes; and it took the passing of my dear mother and matriarch of the Ihetu family, Dame Abigail Ihetu over a decade ago, for me to come to grips with the depth of my father's contributions to boxing and to humanity. The stealth grip of change has also compelled me to delve into my father's involvement in the Biafra war, as I revisit some very painful memories. Over the years, I've learned about my father's remarkable exploits from family, relatives, and strangers-turned-acquaintances—all of whom were eager to share their treasured stories of Dick Tiger's feats inside and outside of the ring. I have heard countless stories of my father's altruism and great grace. I beam with pride every time I hear or read about his patriotism and heroism, as displayed on August 10, 1963, when he bore the weight of an entire nation on his shoulders as he dueled in the first-ever world boxing championship event to be held in Africa. It remains an epochal landmark in Africa's sports history.

My childhood conjures warm memories of my dad's jokes, throaty laughter, his generosity, and his loving and caring nature. The carefree days my siblings and I spent with him remain priceless.

This production is history brought back to life, in a screenplay. It is a labor of love, and my golden opportunity to document Dick Tiger's audacious life for posterity. Come journey with me into his state of mind through peak and valleys. Witness his stoicism, courage, and bravery during those defining moments in Nigeria's history. I hope that Dick Tiger's life serves as a lightning rod against fear and self-doubt for generations to come.

Cast of Characters

(The characters in bold type represent the main characters)

ABIGAIL IHETU: Dick Tiger's wife, the "wind beneath his wings." Her invaluable encouragement and support enabled Dick Tiger to reach greater heights in his remarkable boxing career.

BOBBY DIAMOND: Dick Tiger's representative in Britain. He assisted Jack Solomons in coordinating the Tiger-Fullmer fight in Ibadan.

CHIEF J. M. UDOCHI: Nigeria's ambassador to the United States, who was instrumental in making the fight at home a reality.

CHIEF JOSEPH MODUPE JOHNSON (JMJ): The ebullient and amiable minister of sports in Nigeria, whose vision engineered the successful staging of Africa's first-ever world championship bout in Ibadan, Nigeria.

CHIEF OKEUGO: An oppressive warrant chief.

CHIEF S. O. ADEBO: Nigeria's ebullient and eloquent permanent representative to the United Nations (UN).

DICK TIGER: Also called, Diki, before he became a champion Nigerian boxer and the reigning world middleweight boxing champion.

DICK TIGER Sr: Older Dick Tiger; retired three-time world boxing champion. He is the chief narrator of events in this story.

DR. NNAMDI AZIKIWE: A charismatic leader; he was the governor-general of the Nigerian Federation from 1950 to 1964.

EJIATU REBECCA IHETU: Affectionately called "Taatu." She is Dick Tiger's mother and the matriarch of the Ihetu family.

FIGHT-AT-HOME COMMITTEE SPOKESPERSON: Vocalized the intent and interest(s) of the committee to the Nigerian public.

FOREIGN REPORTER

GENE FULLMER: A champion American boxer who challenged Dick Tiger for the world middleweight championship crown.

GODWIN, NELSON, and CHINAKA: Dick Tiger's siblings.

Gordy "Goldsmith" Uzoaru: Dick Tiger's childhood friend, and a boxing enthusiast. He boxed in the amateur division.

HARRY LEVINE, NORMAN ROTHSCHILD, and MARK RHODES: Boxing promoters who aggressively bid to host the Tiger-Fullmer III Fight.

HOGAN "KID" BASSEY: Featherweight world boxing champion from Nigeria; he is the second African to win a world boxing title.

JACK SOLOMONS: A world-renowned British boxing promoter, who was charged with the audacious task of staging the first-ever world boxing championship bout on African soil.

JIMMY AUGUST: Dick Tiger's trainer in America. Though heavyset, he is endowed with superb training skills.

MARV JENSEN: Gene Fullmer's manager. He performs the same role for Gene Fullmer that Jones does for Dick Tiger.

MESSENGER: A messenger in the Oloko native court.

EBERE: Dick Tiger's personal assistant.

MR. TALADE and **MR. WULITE**: Members of the Nigerian delegation to San Francisco, California, for the first Tiger versus Fullmer fight.

NWANYERUWA, IKONNIA, NWANNEDIA: Militant women. They fight against the oppressive and unfair policies of the colonial British overlords.

PARADE OF SCHOOLCHILDREN: They sing praises of Dick Tiger's duel with Gene Fullmer.

PRESSMAN

REPORTER #1 and REPORTER #2

RICHARD JR.: Dick Tiger's first son, who was named after him.

RING ANNOUNCER

SANGOGBEMI and SANGODIRAN: Rain doctors hired by the Nigerian minister of sports.

SIR ALHAJI ABUBAKAR TAFAWA BALEWA: A powerful legislator and the first and only prime minister of the Federal Republic of Nigeria.

TONY VAIRO: Managed Dick Tiger's career in Liverpool after Tiger lost his first manager, Peter Banasko.

UGBOAJA: Dick Tiger's father.

UMEZE NNOGBUO: Ugboaja's kinsman. He grieved Ejiatu after Ugboaja's death.

WILFRED "JERSEY" JONES: Dick Tiger's American manager. He managed Dick Tiger's training routine and ensured that he had the required diet, training, and focus to win fights.

WOMEN'S DANCING GROUP: They sing and dance in praise of Dick Tiger's feats with Gene Fullmer in the roped ring.

Act One

(*It is early morning in the commercial city of Aba. The Nigerian civil war had ended a year before, and Tiger is home relaxing in his palatial living room. He is sitting in a recliner chair, head thrust backwards; he seems in a jovial mood surrounded by his wife, Abigail, his brothers, Godwin, Nelson, Chinaka, and his good friend, Gordy "Goldsmith." At this impromptu gathering, Dick Tiger bares his soul regarding his family, and some of his fights inside, and outside of the ring.*)

DICK TIGER SR, *grimacing as he tries to sit up.* My brothers, (*pauses*) Gordy, my good friend, you are all welcome. It is great to see you! (*Teasing Chinaka*) You dared to leave the village? (*They laugh.*)

ABIGAIL, *subdued, but tries to be upbeat.* (*She greets each of her brothers- in- law.*) De'm Goddy, De'm Chinaka, De'm Nelson, you are all welcome. Please how are your wives, my dear sisters-in-law? I hope they're doing alright together with the children.

CHINAKA, GODWIN, and NELSON. We are all fine.

ABIGAIL *to Goldsmith.* You're welcome in our home, Sir. How are Mama Emma and the kids doing?

GOLDSMITH. Aby, they're fine, thank you. I'll certainly relay your greetings to them.

ABIGIAL. Yes. Please do. Thank you.

(Tiger's brothers, Chinaka, Nelson, and Godwin, speak a localized or broken English called pidgin.)

NELSON , *cheerfully.* Diki, you sure dey look better than the last time we see you.

GODWIN, *agreeing with Nelson.* Yes, Diki, *(Jokingly)* You been exercise to look good, hah?

(Tiger, once in top shape with a ribbed physique and bulging, hard biceps now seems worn by a dilapidating illness yet radiates the aura of nobility and quiet strength.)

DICK TIGER SR., *perking up.* Then it must be that Abigail's soups, saturated *(Demonstrating)* with the good veggies— bitter-leaf, oha, uziza, ukazi, utazi, are really doing my body good. *(They laugh.)*

CHINAKA. Everyone in the village greets you, Diki. They—

DICK TIGER SR., *interjecting.* And you *(Pointing)* Chinaka, for you to leave the comforts of your farm, *(Animatedly)* the endless chirping of birds, the cock crows at dawn, and in between *(Grinning)* is much, and I appreciate you for that.

CHINAKA, *smiling.* Taatu sends her warm regards. She and everyone in the village is thinking about you. They said to tell you to be strong, that they are praying for you to heal fast. *(Shuffling a duffle bag towards himself, he quickly brings out a small package.)* Here are some more of the good leaves from the village. Veggies for more strength—ugu, bitter-leaf, oha, some more uziza, and utasi. *(He also hands some to Nelson and Godwin.)*

GOODWIN. Ewooh. Thank you.

NELSON. Thank you so much. *(Pointing at Abigail.)* Aby, our wife, you always dey look as good as ever! *(The others agree.)*

ABIGAIL, *blushing.* Thank you so much, sirs. I appreciate the compliment, my husbands. Dem Chinaka, God bless you for the gifts. Please, let me go into the kitchen and prepare breakfast for you. Some oatmeal with bread and tea is okay for you?

NELSON, *waving his hand.* Please, we are not Oyibo (Caucasean), Aby, just get us some fufu. We go like to taste some of the delicious, healthy soup that you serve our brother, Diki.

CHINAKA. Yes, o! Please, our wife, get us a healthy serving of garri or pounded yam with ogbono or egwushi soup and lots of the good vegetables.

GODWIN. No tea or coffee-biscuit. We want real food. *(Laughter)*

GOLDSMITH. Yes, Madam, I wouldn't mind some of the egwushi soup, too. Thank you.

ABIGAIL, *smiling, nodding politely.* No problem, Sirs. I will make some pounded yam with oha soup mixed with egwushi. Does that sound good to you?

GODWIN, CHINAKA, and NELSON. Eyiooh! Thank you so much. *(She leaves.)*

DICK TIGER SR. *(Turns, calling out to her over his shoulder.)* Please take it easy, Aby, sweetheart. Get the maids to help. *(Turning to his brothers)* Aby worries so much about me, my health, and about our young children—all eight of them. *(Pauses)* She is a very strong and intelligent woman, and I thank God every day for bringing her into my life.

CHINAKA. She is a good woman—a rare gem. *(They promptly agree.)*

NELSON. She will be all right. You will be all right.

DICK TIGER SR. I could never have accomplished so much without a woman of her caliber on my side. I remember when she came to join me in London. She brought back laughter and hope into my life. *(Pause)* Before then, I had lost my first four fights, starting with Alan Dean in 1955, *(Quickly)* but the next year when I met Alan, I defeated him, and won the next four fights *(Trailing off)* two of those by knockouts!

(They are startled momentarily by the chirping of young voices, when some of Tiger's older children troop in to greet them.)

RICHARD JR., VICTORIA, CHARLES, and JUSTINA, *excitedly.* Papa, M'pa, *(My Papa)* good morning, Sir!

DICK TIGER SR., *shifting in his chair.* My children, good morning.

Did you sleep well? *(Beaming)*

CHORUS. Yes, sir! Yes, Papa.

RICHARD JR., *excitedly.* Uncle Gordy Goldsmith, Uncle Nelson, Uncle Godwin, Uncle Chinaka, welcome. *(They all take turns gleefully greeting their uncles.)*

NELSON, GODWIN, and CHINAKA. Good morning!

GOLDSMITH. Good to see that you all are doing well!

GODWIN: I hear that you are doing well in school too.

CHORUS. Yes, Sir. Yes, Sir.

NELSON. Your mother also said that you help take care of your sister, Grace, and the younger ones. Keep up the good work, okay? *(They nod in agreement.)*

DICK TIGER SR., *smiling warmly.* They are very good young ladies and gentlemen. *(Deepens voice)* Now, go on my darlings. Eat your breakfast, and wash up. Okay? *(They nod, and leave as rowdily as they came.)*

GOLDSMITH, *smiles.* Very agile and smart children, like their papa! *(Pause)* Diki, you had mentioned Alan Dean. Didn't you fight him, like five or six times?

DICK TIGER SR. Yes. We fought five times, between 1955 and 1957. He beat me twice, and I beat him for the third time in our last match in December 1957, just a few months after I beat the indefatigable Terry Downes.

GOLDSMITH: Yes! Everybody remembers that match with Terry Downes! *(Laughing.)* You beat him so bad that when one of the reporters asked him who he'd fight next, he said...

DICK TIGER SR., *interjecting.* The fool who matched him to fight me! *(They laugh.)* That's who he wanted to fight next. Terry was like that—sharp and witty. He was a skilled boxer too.

GOLDSMITH. In the case of Alan Dean though, it's as if he and his team couldn't stand the thought of you, a rookie from black Africa, daring to challenge and beat their man! *(Laughs.)*

DICK TIGER SR., I probably would have been able to beat Alan on our first match if I had the right training and right diet. Remember how I couldn't get used to the English food or their weather? As if that wasn't bad enough, I was sometimes scheduled for two major tournaments within one month!

CHORUS, *stunned.* What?! How ca—

GODWIN, *interjecting.* Not even the best of the best fighters fit cope with that kind of a crazy schedule!

NELSON, *proudly.* But you showed them your boxing power! You even got the Queen's attention, and you became Member of the Orda of the British Empaya *(Boastfully)* with authority of the Queen Elizabeth II herself. You show them that you are champion!

DICK TIGER SR., *gasping.* Yes, I guess, until the pains came *(Pause)* growing more acute with each fight.

GOLDSMITH. What pain? *(Confused)* Diki, but you had been in lots of matches between your time in Britain and America. It was reported in the news that you felt excruciating pain and fell while working at a museum, and the news came within months after your very last fight. I remember how worried we all were by that broadcast.

NELSON. We very worried. Taatu almost died crying. *(Adamant)* But, Diki, I know you win a lot of fights here in our country, even before you traveled to London. *(Rambling)* You win all your fights here, *(Emphasizing)* starting with Simon Ene in 1952 then Koko Kid. You even win the boxers with some very wild and scary names like, Easy Dynamite, Mighty Joe, Blackie Power, Jean Clod Poison! —

GODWIN, *interjecting.* Don't forget, Super Human Power, and Lion King! *(They cackle.)*

NELSON., *ecstatic.* No be lies! You can't forge this kind of story. *(Quickly)* Diki beat up all of them! All up to his last match here in Nigeria with a boxer named Bolaji Johnson, in 1955, at Glover Memorial Hall, Lagos. He beat Bolaji well-well.

GOLDSMITH. Yes, Diki won all those fighters in Nigeria, except for one young boxer, Tommy—

NELSON. TOMMY West! *(Excitedly)* Yes, Diki fought the champion boxer, Sumonu Akanbi, known as Tommy West, three different times, (*Amazed.*) and he won Diki in all them fights!

GOLDSMITH. Sumonu Akanbi, aka, Tommy west, was another dynamite boxer. He was Nigeria's middleweight champion, and the Collister Belt Winner—a very good boxer, to beat Tiga three times.

NELSON. Is a pity he died so young age, only twenty-two years old. He died few months after he win fight against Diki, to retained his Nigerian middleweight boxing championship.

GOLDSMITH, *incredulously.* Diki, you couldn't have continued boxing in Britain and later in America, winning all those matches with some of the best in the business like, (*Rambling excitedly.*) Pat McAteer, Gene Armstrong, Joey Archer, Wilf Greave, Randy Sandy, Rubin "Hurricane" Carter, Andy Kendall, the Spider Webb, Jose Torres, Frankie Depaula, Gene Fullmer, Gene, "The Cyclone" Fullmer—

GODWIN., *interjecting.* Don't forget, Joey Giardello. They fight each other four times. Diki won two times; he won two also. (*Pauses, and eyes the others.*) Wait, *shifting in his seat.* We talking boxing matches here, when Diki just talk about the pain he started feeling a long, long time before the radio news. (*Empathetically.*) Diki, I'm so sorry to hear this now, but you win all those great fighters carrying pain around? Please, my dear brother, what cause this pain? When actually it start?

(*A maid walks in with a jug filled with freshly squeezed orange juice and some glass cups. She sets the jug in a center-table, gently lays a glass cup beside each of the men and leaves promptly. The men take turns filling their cups with the freshly squeezed juice, as they chat.*)

CHINAKA, *gently.* Diki, when did this pain start in your body? I feel so bad about this. You mean the pain didn't start first when you working in museum, as them tell us on radio?

DICK TIGER SR., *clears his throat,* No. I had felt a stinging pain while training for the fight with Emile Griffith, to retain my middleweight crown in 1966. It was also about the same time when the civil war was looming.

NELSON, *pressing,* What did the doctors tell you?

DICK TIGER SR., *hesitatingly.* I didn't go to the doctor. Because I wanted to win that fight, I ignored the pain. Bore it for so long that I didn't feel it anymore, but—

GOLDSMITH, *interjecting.* But it was there.

DICK TIGER SR. I am not proud about it. *(Sighing.)* I lost that fight, and the middleweight crown. *(Fidgeting)* The sting of the pain kept increasing, and I tried my hardest to stifle it in order to enable me campaign for the light heavyweight championship against Jose Torres. *(Pauses.)* I fought Jose later that same year and won it.

GODWIN, *continuing,* Then, you go to the doctors?

DICK TIGER SR., *frowning.* The Biafra war had started, and I needed to get home. *(Struggling)* You know, just to make sure Abigail and the children and the rest of the family were all right. *(Pause)* When I witnessed firsthand the hunger, starvation, bombings, killings, I blocked off the raging pain. *(Quickly)* I had to fight Abraham Tonica right then in Port Harcourt, to raise money to help alleviate the pain and suffering that I witnessed in our people's fight for freedom against oppression and suppression. *(Shaking his head slightly.)* The pain was gone then, but for a little while.

GOLDSMITH, *stunned.* Diki was logging pain around, hoping it would leave miraculously?

DICK TIGER SR. No. Not really. *(Searching his thoughts.)* You know I have lived a tough life, and with my stringent trainings and fights, I had vicariously built up a good tolerance threshold for pain.

GODWIN. So, my brother, you fight Jose Torres again and win, then you fight Rouse the same year?

GOLDSMITH and NELSON. Yes!

CHINAKA, *shocked.* And you won again. And all that time you had this pain parked in your body? You cannot tell is there?

DICK TIGER SR., I didn't feel any stinging pain any more than my body is used to, until after my bout with Bob Foster. After that TKO, pain surged through my body like never before. It was like an avalanche of pain. The intensity of it is indescribable. *(Snickering)* Now I know how the fighters I've knocked out felt. *(Pause)* But once again, I was able to overpower and overcome the pain for some time. War was now raging in my homeland, and our people needed my help. Aside from needing food and clothing, they also needed training in combat, to live to fight another day.

CHINAKA, *softly.* Did you tell Aby? About the pain?

DICK TIGER SR., *shaking his head gently.* No. I did not want to add to her burden. *(Pause)* She already has to raise our children without me home.

GOLDSMITH, *sympathetically.* So, Diki, that means you harbored excruciating pain for most of nine fights, since after your fight with Griffith in 1966? That's astonishing!

DICK TIGER SR., *chuckles.* I don't know how I was able to manage *(Putting three fingers up.)* three wars at the same time—

GODWIN and NELSON, *confused.* Three wars?

NELSON. What three wars?

DICK TIGER SR., *animatedly.* I was managing the pain, the title fights, and the war that was raging in our country. *(Pensively)* Even after I suffered that devastating TKO from Foster, I didn't give up. I couldn't. I needed the purse money *(pauses)* so I could continue to help.

GOLDSMITH. Correct. You went on to fight four more times, winning three out of the four, even bagging the coveted Ring Magazine's, "Fight of the Year" Award for your showdown with Frankie Depaula! Bravo! *(They cheer.)*

DICK TIGER SR., *struggles to smile.* Thank you. I had to manage the pain, and it took all of my strength to hold off that pain. But I had to. There was war raging in my beloved homeland, and my people were dying in the hundreds, daily! I couldn't feel my own bodily pains, *(Stubbornly)* but the only pain I could feel was the pain of our people of Biafra. *(Pause)* I had to make efforts to get help—food, clothes, and ammunition— through my briefings with the foreign press. I wanted the world to know about the persecutions and killings. *(Pause)* Some said, "Forget about that war, Tiger. Move your family to America, win more fights, and live happy!" *(Sternly)* I say, no! Without Biafra, the championship title was no good to me. I had to throw both my middleweight and light heavyweight into the mix to abate the persecution and killings of my people.

ALL, *stomping and singing (2x.)*

Nzogbu! Nzogbu! Enyimba! Enyi! Nzogbu! Enyimba! Enyi! (Battle-cry)

Fighter Jets

DICK TIGER SR., *gently shifting in the recliner.* I was hesitant to move my family away from our homeland, but I received sensitive information from certain quarters, *(Pointing)* including pressure from you guys, my family members, and Aby especially, to move the children away from the siege in the country. (*Struggling*) I had to bring them to America, anyway, or I wouldn't have been able to focus to train and win fights. (D*eepening his voice.*) I am a true son of the soil. My heart has always been, and shall remain with my country. *(Pauses)* No matter where I go around the world; no matter how beautiful those places are, I always yearned for my country. It is the most beautiful to me. *(Pauses)* Even after I was diagnosed wit*h* cancer, my doctors and everyone else I know, in all good intentions urged me to stay back in America for treatment. *(Pauses)* The war had ended and there were a lot of uncertainties about the way I may be received if I returned to our country right after the war; and judging from the fact that I was a highly prized asset in the propaganda war that was played out during the civil disorder.

CHIINAKA. Yes. We no want you come back then, bcos we no no how the Nigeria govment will treat you.

GODWIN. We fear say them go want to catch you and throw you prison, or even harm you.

DICK TIGER SR., *stoically*. I considered all of that, (*emphasizing*) but I just needed to come home. (*Gently shifting in his seat*) I needed to return my wife and children to our roots.

GOLDSMITH. That's when you went to the Nigerian Embassy in New York, to-

DICK TIGER SR., *affirming*. To confirm that I would be eligible for the amnesty granted by the Nigerian Government to return home (Pauses) I was later reassured of a safe passage into the country by the Nigerian Ambassador, Edwin Ogeve-Ogbu, at the United Nations. *(Halting)* Even though my travel documents were seized upon my return to the country, I was elated. *(Pauses)* For me, there is no place like home; and if I am to die from this ailment, I'd rather die in my country than in a foreign land.

NELSON, *reassuring*. You be a treasure child of we country nah. You be national hero, and you must come back to your country. (*Pause*) Everybody dey so happy and proudly when you come back to us.

DICK TIGER SR. The war was disastrous for the entire country and had bastardized our fledgling democracy, (*admonishing*) but injustice should have no place in the country. *(Pauses)* If we are to move forward as a united and progressive country, then there must be justice and equity for all citizens of the country. *(Clearing his throat)* I wish there was another way we could have quelled the prevailing injustice and discord, without resorting to war. (*Pauses*) That weighed heavily on my mind so much that after the war; (*pausing*) in my very last fight, I needed to let the world know right there on the boxing stage, that the Biafra war was over! (*Shaking his head slightly.*) No more killings. No more destruction.

GOLDSMITH, *excitedly.* I remember that moment right after the fight. The announcer—I think named Dundee—had interviewed Griffith first and then came to you. The crowd cheered! He asked you (*Imitating*), "So Dick, what about the future?" You replied, "About the war in my country, I am so happy that we are one again. I will go back to my country, see my family, my people."

DICK TIGER SR., *sternly.* But we also know that it will take a concerted effort on all sides in the war to ensure that there is equity and fairness in both the political, and legislative arms of government. (*Visually searching their faces.*) I envision it the only way that peace and unity can be actualized in Nigeria. (*Swallowing hard.*) Our children and grandchildren must be able to lift their hands to their chests in the pledge of allegiance to the Nigerian flag, without reservations! (*Pause*) Only when they can pledge allegiance and sing exultations to our great country of Nigeria without a shred of reservation, will we know, without a doubt, that as a nation we are headed for true greatness. That is my hope.

(*They all stand, shouting, "Yes, yes!"*)

CHINAKA. That is all what we pray for, my broda.

DICK TIGER SR. Thank you very much for the vote of confidence, my brothers. (*Straining*) It's just that I have been feeling a (*hesitating*) a little uneasy and (*mumbles*) sorry for myself lately. It still bothers me that millions of people lost their lives in that war. And—

NELSON, *interrupting.* No. Why? Don't talk like that, Diki, (*pauses*) you are loved very much. (*Excitedly*) the greatest boxer from Nigeria and Africa! You went from bottle-picking boy to world champion!

GODWIN. Diki, there's no reason for you to doubt yourself or feel bad. Our childhood in the backwoods of Eastern Nigeria, bottle-pickin' on the streets, fist fightin' for water at Aba city water pumps, and other small jobs, no make you hopeless, or want commit suiide. No! You give a lot people hope about tomorrow. *(Pause)* Your small beginning no prevents you from becoming one of the greater boxing champions of all time! We be so proud of you, and *(feeling overwhelmed.)* in fact, most of the worlds admire you.

DICK TIGER SR., *suddenly talkative.* It was not easy, but I turned the deficits of our environment into benefits, with my talent for receiving and returning mayhem, *(laughing softly)* honed on the streets of Aba and perfected in the roped rings of Europe and America. It wasn't easy at all! (*Halting briefly*) In Britain and America, I was pitted against only the toughest, and sometimes the craftiest of contenders in the sweet science of boxing. *(Reflecting)* I remember how dejected I felt losing the middleweight championship to Joey Giardello right after I had retained it boxing Fullmer before my people in Ibadan. After that fight, *(emphatically)* Giardello promptly agreed before the press, to grant me the chance to regain the championship. He assured me a rematch within months of my losing the championship crown to him, (*Shifting*) but it was not to be so!

NELSON. Yes .*(Pauses)* You two no box again until almost tw—

DICK TIGER SR., *punctuating each word.* Two years! (*Slightly shaking his head*) Joey is a nice guy, but he dances around the truth a bit. I was fuming mad!

GODWIN., *smirks.* He be very afraid of fighting you nah, like many of them other fighters! He be smart. (*Snickering*) He knows that Diki be good person, but in the ring; as soon as he hear that bell, kpaam! Him only focus na just to destroy his opponent!

DICK TIGER SR. He kept promising, and equivocating, but I didn't sit around waiting. In the time between losing the crown to Giardello and waiting for him to actually do a rematch, I fought bouts with the likes of Jose Gonzalez, Juan Carlos, and Rubin Carter. I won all of them except for Joey Archer, who decisioned me in the tenth round of our match.

GOLDSMITH. You also fought with Gene Fullmer's brother—

DICK TIGER SR. Don Fullmer. Yes, I fought Don too. *(Swallowing hard.)* I worked extra hard to win all those fights, to remain a relevant pick to box Giardello for the middleweight championship. *(Continuing)* At a press conference in one of those grief-stricken months waiting for Giardello, a reporter had the nerve of insinuating that, maybe Giardello is just waiting until I get old? Until I lose my edge? Ha! I didn't appreciate that at all. I clapped back, stating that Giardello is as old as I!

GOLDSMITH. Yes, that's right. He is!

DICK TIGER SR., *growling.* A tiger never loses his hunger! *(Pause)* When I finally got the chance to claim the championship back, I did not relent. I unleashed my most punishing shots, and trapped Giardello from his trademark running, dodging, and backtracking all over the ring. I—

GOLDSMITH, *interjecting.* Yes. Sometimes he just strolls around the ring, twirling his arms like a bicycle wheel! *(They laugh.)*

DICK TIGER SR., *tries to demonstrate.* I methodically let my right hand pave the way for my lethal left hook to deliver shots to the torso with complete gusto and relish, for the full fifteen rounds!

GOLDSMITH, *excitedly.* He knew you had him!

DICK TIGER SR. I knew I'd won, even before the cards were read. *(Grinning)* It was a sweet revenge; one of my most gratifying bouts, ever.

GODWIN. And I know you fight him four times in all.

Look what you did, Tiger

DICK TIGER SR. He won on two occasions. *(Incredulously)* Aaah, these days you get a boxing championship title by running away *(mumbles)*. I didn't train to be a runner. *(Pauses)* Regardless of the caliber of the fighter in all of my matches, I trained tirelessly. From each misstep and fall, I bounced back, refined my skills in order to beat down the next opponent.

ALL, *excitedly*. Tiga! Tiga! Tiga!

DICK TIGER SR., *smiling; weighs each word*. I ruled the world of professional boxing not once or twice, but three times—when I became the British Empire middleweight champion, then middleweight boxing champion, of the world, and later the light heavyweight boxing champion, of the world. *(Quickly)* I glorify God Almighty!

(They all stand in ovation with each giving him the gentlest pat on the back.)

ALL, *shouting.* Glory to Orisa (God)! Hallelujah! Hallelujah!

DICK TIGER SR., *blushing, he motions them to sit.* Please my brothers, please sit. Thank you so much.

GOLDSMITH. YOU are still the greatest, and humblest of all the big boxers! Take for example, the great Mohammed Ali.

NELSON and GODWIN, *snickering.* Ewooh! (Gosh!)

NELSON. He can brag! Don't you see how he walk *(demonstrates)* Strutting around the boxing ring like—

GODWIN, *quickly.* Like the ring is his parlor (living room)! *(They laugh.)* Ali!

Ali!

GOLDSMITH. Ali is one of the greatest fighters, just like you are, Diki. A lot of people like both your styles for different reasons *(Pauses)* you, for your humility and generosity, and Ali *(Pause)* mmm—

DICK TIGER SR., *interjecting.* I know *(Pause)*, but it's not that. *(Trying to steady his voice.)* It's just that I keep thinking and stressing about my children and Abigail, wondering what will become of them when I am gone.

GOLDSMITH, *sorrowfully.* Oh *(Pause)* don't worry yourself. They will be fine. They want you to get well soon. *(Deepens his voice.)* Did you hear from the government yet, about your application to have your passport returned so you could travel for the operation>?

DICK TIGER SR., *sighs*. They refused. Said I was still a risk to the country, because I supported Biafra and gave them a bad reputation before the world.

GOLDSMITH. But the war is over *(Exasperated)*. The country won. *(Pause)* Even the Snr. secessionist officers have all affirmed and pledged allegiance to the Federal Military Government of Nigeria! Biafrans are defeated. We do not have no more liver or muscles right now to make war. We are now at their mercy just trying to survive on their terms!

NELSON., *incensed, hitting his hands on the center table*. But it can't be like that! We no coss the war—

Goldsmith., *quickly*. Besides, despite the incessant massacre of the Igbos in the northern states, we didn't want a war, so the meeting in Aburi, Ghana, to give peace a chance!

NELSON, *interjecting*. Yes! To give peace a chance! *(frustrated)* But them no gree! Them lie. We show, by Aburi, that we wan peace and unify in Nigeria, but them go there go do everything like play, like play. *(Pauses)* Wetin them wan make we do? *(Pauses)* Na we people them chase out. So, now ndi Igbo no get businesses! No money! No house! Ewuuu! Na we dey hurt nah. Our childrens hungry and crying nah. *(In disbelief)* And them think say we go go dia play? And dance around on we children's and family's sufferings? Mbanu! (Of course not!)

GOLDSMITH. The coup, counter coup and resulting pogrom committed against the Igbos in the northern states obviously left both sides, Igbos and the northern states on the Federal side, harboring a lot of resentment and mistrust. *(Pause)* At the meeting in Aburi, the leadership on both sides reached consensus *(nodding)* that were agreeable to both sides, in what's now called, the Aburi Accord. *(Quickly)* However, like

Nelson said, *(sighs)* at the drop of a hat, *(Raising both hands in despair)* the Federal side did a total U turn!

DICK TIGER SR. They backtracked on agreements reached at Aburi that would have helped usher in peace and stability to the country at that time. (*Pause*) one of the major agreements of the accord was that the use of arms should never be considered in resolving issues within the country, but sadly, the tenets of the accord was derailed by claims and counter-claims, distortion of facts in the agreement, and *(in resignation)* Anyway, *(gently waving his hands)* It's all behind us now. We must move past our grievances if the country is to heal.

NELSON, *incensed.* Na them coss the problem wey drive our country to war! (*To Diki*) And them no gree give you back you passport, Diki? *(Shaking his head)* Mmhu! This life sef, *(flustered)* so them forget all the other great, big things you do for this country befo, eh?

GODWIN. Na them start the war with all the killings, when them go crazy start killing Ndi Igbo in the north. (*Pause*) No be them treat us like old tire, rejects? *(Wrinkling his nose.)* Wetin them want make we do nah? (*Pauses*) If person don't want you and you want leave, wetin wrong that?

CHINAKA. Odi kwa egwu! (Incredible!) Na them start with the bombing and killings! *(Pause.)* If one or two people crazy go cause problems, like stealing or killing, *(shouting)* then you deal with them nah! But, mba! (No!) You go go start shooting and killing everybody? Innocent peoples like that? That is like monsta!

DICK TIGER SR., *putting a hand up.* My brothers, let us keep marching forward. (*Deepening his voice*) The future looks brighter now. The federal government has signed the "No

Victor, No Vanquished" document, which promises that the Igbos, who are the vanquished, will not be abused anymore. It guarantees that we stay as one country, where every citizen of the country will have all their civil rights, without discrimination. (*Waving his hands.*) No more killings. No more kwashiorkor killing babies and children.

Children suffering from kwashiorkor

GOLDSMITH. Things are so bad. (*Shaking his head, snapping his fingers*) Let us hope that what's stipulated in the proclamation will be adhered to (*Looking dejected*). Our people have suffered untold hardships. (*Pause*) Remember what happened when the federal forces tried to gain entrance into the Biafran hinterland, through the bridge near Nsirimo in Umuahia? (*With his eyes he searches their faces, then continues.*) The Biafran soldiers had to break the bridge linking Nsirimo village in Umuahia to Umunwanwa village in Mbaise.

GODWIN. Yes! (*Pouting*) Who fit forget that disasta!

GOLDSMITH, continuing. The Biafran soldiers had to break the bridge! *(Squeezing his face.)* Remember? They did so to prevent the federal forces from gaining entrance into Biafra hinterlands of Okigwe, Owerri and Orlu.

GODWIN, *disgusted, squeezing his face.* Ewuu! All of our peoples trying to run to cross the bridge before e break, all die! Bloody body pieces all inside river! *(Shrugs his shoulders, puts both hands on his head)* Ewuu!

GOLDSMITH, *shrieking.* All of them fell inside the river and were crushed by the iron beams from the damaged bridge. *(Pauses, leans back into his chair.)* Some people say months later they could still hear the piercing cries of those people that drowned. Chai! *(Snapping his fingers)* Aruu! (Abomination!)

CHINAKA, *upset.* It was disasta! A lot of the peoples wey fall inside the water are mosly womens and childrens trying to run to oda side of brige to scape the enemy force. *(Pauses)* It was terribu!

DICK TIGER Sr., *visibly shaken, sighs as he struggles to shift in his seat.* That was one of the most horrific days of the war! *(Pause)* I was at the Biafra Missions in New York when the news was received. That same river, it was reported, retained a red hue, *(Pauses)* color of blood, for days! *(Pause)* Blood of our people that spilled, when they met their doom trying to cross the bridge from Nsirimo to the safety of their homes in Umunwanwa.

GOLDSMITH, *lips trembling.* Sometimes I truly wonder whether that war was a mistake. Every family in Igbo land went through a uniquely awful experience. Too many lives lost. Too many families broken up, and millions of our people rendered homeless and poor. *(Sighs)*

NELSON., *stressing.* Okay! But them had no oda choice than to break the brige! If them no break that brige, the federal fighters for come, marching into Igbo land, and them for kill a lot lot more people than the ones wey die for inside river. (*Getting emotional*) What else you for do when someone is abuse you, even abuse your childrens? *(Quickly)* You fight, very hard! (*Pauses*) Our sojas do the right thing. (*Frowning*) But we know is wrong that a lot people die. I sorry. Yes. *(Pause)* But we must to fight them! For we too want respect, and good life for we families, like them do for they own. But we no just go abuse or kill anybody everybody wey no do us anythin', just to have power? (*Astonished*) For why? *(Turning to Diki.)* Don't worry. You are not going anywhere yet, Diki. We will always look out for each other, like you do for we. That's family. God will show us mercy.

CHORUS. Amen!

Refugees fleeing

DICK TIGER SR., *continuing.* Since after the civil war, the government has seized all of my properties, and I do not know if or when they will return them to me. *(Straining to throw his hands in the air.)* Those are all I have left now to take care of my family. Most of the purse money I made fighting in the ring is gone, gone to the Biafra war *(pause)* fighting to protect my people. *(Sighs)* But I can't complain. I'm not the only one that lost everything.

CHINAKA. I thank God most of we family survived, but I know a lot people in our village die during the war. A lot wives no have husband, and the children no father. *(Pouting)* A lot of the sons die. *(Pauses)* It very, very sad. *(Pauses)* Do you rememba about the disasta bomb and deaths in Ogui near Aba, here? It was terrybu! Human body pieces be everywhere, *(Wrinkling his face.)* Bloody, blood all the places! Bad smell of burn peoples fill the air! Ewuu! It was evil! *(Pause)*

GODWIN. Oh! *(Shrieking)* I rememba it very well! The federal force bring them mighty fireworks to near Aba Oo! *(Mumbles)* The power shellin' been felt even in church! *(Shocked)* At St. Michaels Church, here in Aba. *(Mumbles)* Even the bishop and canons all run faster for life! Chai!

CHINAKA, *continuing.* The bombs destroy a lot, lots of bildings and houses into pieces of dust. People trap in them, crying hard. No help. It was evil! *(Pause)* Painful crying full everywhere. *(Opening his palms to the sky)* Thank you, Orisa, that we be alife to tell this. *(Pauses)* And even the small surviving people propty the government take. Ihe ojo! (Not good!) Is like them seize all propety belongings to all Igbo big men. *(Wistfully)* Do you regret helping Biafra, Diki?

DICK TIGER SR., *emphatically.* No! Chinaka. Why? *(Pause)* I do not regret helping my people in their fight for their dignity, especially not when I witnessed a lot of our people dying senselessly. Ndi Igbo were being massacred by the hundreds daily during the war, and all because they wanted a stop to the marginalization and unfair treatment meted them by a government that they had sworn allegiance to. *(Pauses)* I couldn't turn my back on the untold sufferings and bloodshed. *(Emphatically)* No regrets at all. Maybe, just maybe, there should have been a petition for classified intelligence gathering, from the pilots of the Biafra war. We could then have used the intel to serve as a springboard for brokering peace between the easterners and the government to avert the slaughter of the millions of innocent people. *(Sighs)* But my emotions took over! *(Gently shifting in his recliner.)* While stationed in America, I was bombarded with gruesome pictures of the diabolically orchestrated starvation and slaughter of the Igbos, my people, by the government that was sworn to safeguard and protect their lives and properties. *(Pause)* That was when I volunteered as a lieutenant in the Biafra army. *(Pauses)* Absolutely no agenda on my part. *(Clenching his fist.)* I just needed to help my people. We had been cornered into a hellish position and we needed an exit, *(pause)* and like a skilled boxer cornered in the ring, all you could do and must do is fight and fight hard! *(Unreservedly)* The money I made in the ring didn't mean a lot to me when my people are being persecuted and massacred.

GODWIN. YOU helped a lot, Diki! You save a lot of people lives. You brought in *(Demonstrating)* planeloads of food reliefs and second-hand clothes. *(Bewildered)* Sometimes Diki would even come back home from abroad, with fresh wounds on his face. You fit see the blood-stain bandages wrapped over his bleeding eyebrow, just to come give help to our people. *(Pause)* He even take over part training of our young men, giving them strategy and gorilla warfare tactics to make them combolt ready, and—

NELSON., *correcting.* You mean, he trained them to be combat-ready, for war. *(Quickly).* I don't even think most people in the world know our pain and remem—

DICK TIGER SR., *interjecting.* I grew even more incensed by the escalating war and death toll after I had managed to flee to Lisbon, Portugal with Aby and the children. While there, we received news of the bombing death of Abigail's only brother, Shedrack. *(Heaves a sigh, shakes his head.)* Aby was beside herself with grief! She cried all the time, and would not eat for three days straight! *(Pause)* And I, in turn, became a slave to my emotions. *(Pause)* The war had been brought straight to my doorsteps, and I became like a loose tiger on the prowl for vengeance!

CHINAKA. Yes nah! *(sighs)* So sorry Aby lose her only broda. Chai! We hear it. *(Shaking his head.)* This war ehh!. *(Pause)* War no good at all! See, them lose them only broda and son! Many many other people too. So sorry.

DICK TIGER SR., *pensively.* That was also about the time I was to face Roger Rouse in the roped ring to retain my light heavyweight title. *(Searching their faces with his eyes.)* Do you remember what happened at that match?

NELSON., *quickly.* I know, Mmhmm, it was the only time that you were knocked out in the ring! *(Throwing his hands in the air.)* Howww could youuu allow fellow boxer knock out you like that, Diki? Ewooh! And—

GODWIN., *interjecting.* Only on round fourth! *(Shrugging)* But truly, he be a lot more taller than you, Diki! *(Smirks)* It was like David and Goli—

DICK TIGER SR., *ignoring their quips.* Alright, yes Foster was much younger than me too. *(Shaking his head.)* Roger however, didn't knock me out. Anyway, it was in the match with Roger Rouse that I first wore my Biafran robe to the ring, before the whole world! *(Beaming)* I refused to get up for the match until the Biafran national anthem was played!

Dick Tiger training soldiers

GOLDSMITH, *gratefully.* Yes. Diki, you put everything up for that war; your money, your family life, your boxing, all the things, for our people.

NELSON., *adding.* Don't forget the great award he received from the Queen herself, Elizabeth II *(Animatedly hitting his head.)* Oh, that one pain me! You know what he did, right? *(Pause)* He went and give it back to the Queen! *(Desperately)* Why, Diki? *(Softly)* A lot of our other people kept their own awards they got from the Queen. *(Pauses)* And right after you return that big award in December 1969, the civil war end a few weeks later in January 1970!

DICK TIGER SR., *shrugs.* I know. That was at the height of the war. Too many of our people were dead, or dying, and I couldn't keep it. There was desolation everywhere, and mass graves, unmarked graves, and other atrocities magnified. *(Pause)* I couldn't bear to look at that award, *(Pause)* not when it was reported that the British were supplying ammunition and classified intel used in the pogrom. That award represented to me the bloodshed and sufferings of our people, and I had to send it back on its way.

GODWIN., *looking incredulous,* Diki, you would support the war again? Look, they even seize your school! The first high school in our community you build with your sweating and blood, so that our young youth can get good education *(mumbles)* and they took it, to punish you *(Shaking his head.),* because you want your people free, alive, and well?

CHINAKA., *quickly.* The same govment is also making sure that Diki pay taxes on the school, including all other properties that them took from him. *(Astonished)* How can government ask you pay taxes on something that they take away from you? *(Frowning)* Rubbish!

GOLDSMITH., *sadly.* After all said, it was like fighting a losing battle.

GODWIN and NELSON, *shocked.* What?

GOLDSMITH., *flustered.* Yes! There was not enough artillery for our soldiers. Some of them did not even have boots or uniform to wear to war. There were saboteurs everywhere, against Biafra, even within the army. People were selling out their own people for a cup of cornmeal or a loaf of bread. *(In resignation.)* The war resulted in intense hunger and starvation with hundreds of civilians and soldiers dying daily. *(Halts)* To add salt to the wound, the federal government devalued the Biafra currency, giving a paltry, small change of only twenty pounds *(Shaking his head.)* to each Igbo man, regardless of how many thousands or millions they had in the bank before the drums of war started beating! *(Gently beating his chest.)* We, Ndi Igbo, have always had drive, stamina, determination, and most of us were business owners, *(Pause)* but the war has pushed most of us into poverty.

NELSON. No matter, but we need to fight back! It is the British that supply the big guns to kill us all, and they block every entry at Oguta Lake and Uli Airport from bringin' all things we needed! *(Wringing his hands.)* Even our soldiers have to trek long way with no food or water and carrying only small guns to defend against automatic rifles and heavy artillery! *(Halts)* Whatever them take from Ndi Igbo, e don matter at all! *(Pause)* Them go run, not walk come out of the poverty wey them push them in. Them go run out, sharp sharp! *(Continuing)* E no matter if them take everything from ndi Igbo, them go recovar all! *(At Goldsmith)* You jus talk now say Igbos drive, can stam hunger, and them be big businesses people-----

GODWIN, *interjecting.* Ndi igbo go richer again! Even when govment take all our monies, e no matter. Na God, only, we trust. *(Pause)* Na Orisa we trust. Na em be the Supreme giver of wealth, and wellbeing. *(Looking upwards with palms outstretched)* Orisa di n'igwe, anyi na ekele gi. Chineke nna anyi, nara ekele. Eze, Chineke anyi. Eze nke ndi Eze n'eze, mere anyi ebere, ma gbaghara kwa anyi nmehie anyi. Gozie anyi,Nna, biko. Gozie ezi n'ulo anyi, ma gozie kwa oru aka anyi, onye nwe anyi. Onwe ghi ih I n'apughi ime, Chineke Nna. Ekwe kwala ka ihere megbue anyi wu umu gi. Ihe ndia n'ile k'anyi n'ario gi si te n'aha Jesus Christ wu onye nwe anyi. Amen!

[Translation: Our God in heaven, King of kings and Lord of Lords, we thank you for our lives. We ask for forgiveness of our sins, Lord, even as we ask for total healing, and restoration of your blessings in our lives, Father, God. There is nothing too much for you to do. We ask that you bless us, Father, God. Bless our families, and bless the works of our hands. May we never be confounded, Lord, God. Have mercy upon us, and receive our prayers oh Lord, we ask in Jesus' mighty and redeeming name. Amen!]

Dick Tiger Sr., Chinaka, Nelson, and Goldsmith, *chorus.* Amen!

DICK TIGER SR. Godwin nwanne'm, thank you so much for that short but powerful prayer.

GOLDSMITH, *interjecting.* Some people forget that God is Omniscient. He hears all prayers, short or long. The Bible tells us too, that even before we pray, God already knows our needs so, He has already heard this prayer and will perfect all that concerns us.

All, (*Thunderously loud)* Amen!

CHINAKA., *sensing Tiger's mood.* Alright, beautiful prayer, but enough of the war talk, please! (*Teasing)* You know Diki can be hotheaded. Afterall, he was born in a time of war, but a different kind of war—

NELSON and GODWIN., *animatedly.* The Women's war!

GODWIN. Right here inside Aba. In the year of 1929 *(Pointing at Tiger.),* the year of your birth. Tell us about that war -- fighter!

CHINAKA. Yes, please, our brother, you be the main story teller, tell us about that women's war that happen in year of you birth!

DICK TIGER SR., *animated.* Sure. I'll be delighted to. (*Pause)* I also cannot wait to tell you about another of my all-time favorite period, in the course of my boxing career—

(Abigail walks in, with two maids carrying trays of piping hot food and drinks. The maids lay the bowls of food and drinks unto the dining room table, and leave with the trays.)

ABIGAIL., *smiling.* Thank you for your patience, Sirs. As requested, here's some egwushi soup with pounded yam, and yes, I was sure to add lots and lots of the good veggies!

GODWIN, *sniffing.* Ewooh! This smells and looks delicious! Thank you, madam.

CHINAKA, *rubbing his hands together.* Our wife, God bless you. I guess we can let the story wait until after we eat.

GODWIN. Supported! Aby, thank you so much.

NELSON. Am very hungry and can't wait to get the pounded yam and the egwushi-veggie soup to meet in my mouth! *(They laugh.)*

ABIGAIL. You are quite welcome, Sirs. *(To Tiger)* Di'm, (My husband) please try and eat some as well.

DICK TIGER SR. Thank you, sweetheart. I will. *(She exits.)*

(Before digging into the meal, they pray. After the meal, they continue from where they'd stopped.)

GODWIN. That was some delicious meal! Thank you to you and our wife, Aby. May God continue to bless the hands that make this meal possible for us to enjoy!

CHORUS. Amen!

DICK TIGER SR., *dramatically.* My brothers, Gordy, my dear friend, relax while I tell you about the Women's War—

NELSON. You mean, a time when the oyibos (Caucasians) stepped on *(mumbles)* scorpions! *(They cackle.)*

GOLDSMITH. Yes *(Jokingly)*, when they pulled the tiger by the tail, tampering with the women's pots and pans!

DICK TIGER SR., *clearing his throat.* Now, listen and learn, as I narrate the story of how it all happened with, I dare say, the brave women. *(Excitedly)*

In the year 1929, the same year as my birth, British colonial authorities bit off more than they could chew when they enacted a tax law to swell the coffers of the colonial government. Their new law encountered tremendous resistance from the market women in the southeastern region of the British Protectorate of Nigeria. Women and children had been exempted from taxation, but the new "reassessment of the tax law" included a reassessment of the taxable wealth of the market women too! Prices of locally made goods, which the women sell, were falling, while heavy customs duties were imposed on imported materials they depend on for daily use. With the colonial policies threatening and weakening the women's social and economic status, the market women made several attempts to hold a dialogue with the administrators but were shunned; therefore, they took matters into their own hands to curb what they perceived as the excesses of an unjust and insensitive foreign government. The colonizers maintain control indirectly, through local chiefs called warrant chiefs. These chiefs dispatch court messengers to individual families to ascertain the value of the possessions of those families. Okeugo is one such corrupt warrant chief. He refused to heed the advice of fellow warrant chiefs to relax the enforcement of the unfair tax law. As a result, he met with a most unfortunate reprisal when the militant market women attacked.

SCENE TWO

DICK TIGER SR. Earlier in the week, Chief Okeugo addressed a gathering of messengers in his office at the Oloko native court. The courtroom is adorned with pictures of colonial rulers and His Majesty, King George V. Okeugo, is a tall, muscular, and young man, with a scar near his left eyebrow. He wore a red cap with a bird's feather protruding upward, khaki shorts, and a T-shirt, with a traditional wrap draped over one shoulder and hanging to his knees.

CHIEF OKEUGO., *shrieking; pointing at each of the men.* Messengers of His Majesty's court! We have not met the required tax quota to enable the Honorable Captain Hill to effectively carry out His Majesty's wishes in our province! You are hereby directed to comb through (*Mimicking the action with his hands.*) all the houses and compounds in Oloko! (*Eyes big and angry*) Enter every taxable item into your notebooks—Man's! Woman's! Child's! Livestock and other valuables! (*He twirls a stick in his hands.*) Any subject who resists your authority resists His Majesty's orders and must be punished! (*He motions them to leave.*) Now go!

(*The messengers scamper in different directions. As they leave, he calls out to them. They halt.*)

CHIEF OKEUGO. Take a measurement of every farm! (*They nod.*) Count their cash crops and their yam heaps! We must meet these very reasonable demands of our venerable masters! (*Working himself up into a frenzy, he wrings his hands, crushing the stick he holds between his hands.*) Go! Go! (*They begin to leave. He fires a final warning.*) Anyone who fails to cooperate must be made to regret it!

(*As they leave, Okeugo peers at the crushed pieces of wood in his hands. Sighing, he takes off his red cap and self-consciously sinks into a chair.*)

Scene Three

DICK TIGER SR. One of Chief Okeugo's messengers, a shifty-looking young man, upon hearing the bleating of goats and other livestock, bolted into the residence of a widow, Nwanyeruwa, while she is scantily dressed and doing chores around her house.

MESSENGER: (*With a pen point positioned on his notepad, eyes searching the area, haughtily questions Nwanyeruwa.*) Nwanyiaa! (Hey woman!) How many goats and sheeps do you have?

(*A vivacious woman, she ignores him continuing with her chores. He walks right in front of her and stands, looking her squarely in the face.*)

MESSENGER, *demanding.* Nwanyi! (Woman!) Count your people, goats, sheeps, and other valuables. How many do you have?

NWANYERUWA, *angrily.* Your widowed mama was counted?

MESSENGER, *eyes big and angry, grabs her by the throat.* What did you say? Are you mad?

NWANYERUWA, *promptly grabs his crotch and screams.* Ewoo oh! Ewoo oh! Him wan killi me oo! Him wan killi me oo!

(*A squabble ensues, and there are more harsh exchanges. The commotion attracts the attention of some neighbors who come to her aid to boot the messenger out of their compound.*)

DICK TIGER SR. When news of Nwanyeruwa's ordeal confirmed the district office's intentions of imposing the new tax levy, the market women were up in arms. Their leaders organized and mobilized them by passing a palm leaf to each woman in the localities as a symbol of solidarity in a time of trouble. The next day, women from Owerri, Calabar, and Umuahia, numbering more than a thousand, some elderly, walking with branches of trees for crutches, converged at Chief Okeugo's residence in Oloko. The situation escalated into a frenzy as the women looted and burned Chief Okeogu's residence to the ground!

SCENE FOUR

DICK TIGER SR. As the women's uprising in protest of the new tax levy continued, the turbulence was a world away from Ugboaja and Ejiatu Ihetu, who held me, their third child, christened, Richard (Dick Tiger) Iherigbo. There was rejoicing as relatives and well-wishers celebrated this latest addition to the Ihetu family.

(*Sitting with family and friends in the shade of a mango tree facing his home, Ugboaja, a wrestler—bold, plum-skinned, and stocky—takes a calabash cup and fills it with palm wine. With the other hand, he picks up his newborn.*)

UGBOAJA. *Oya*! Everybody, get you cup of sweet palm wine and let say thank you for Orisa!

(*Everybody scrambles for a cup and fills it with wine. They stand, raising their cups to the sky. Still holding the baby, Ugboaja pours libation to Orisa, the god of their ancestors. As he pours drops of wine from the cup onto the dusty red soil intermittently, he speaks.*)

UGBOAJA, *looking toward the sky*. Orisa di n'elu, (God in heaven) I thank you for my son's life today and his life in the future!

RELATIVES. *Offor*!

(*He pours a few more drops on the ground and speaks.*)

UGBOAJA. Orisa di n'elu, when the many, many headaches of life pain him, please give him power to fight and fight till he wins!

RELATIVES. Offor! (Yes).

(*Still standing, he puts the half-full cup down and motions for his guests to sit. He walks out from under the shade of the tree, and with both hands, he lifts his newborn to the heavens.*)

UGBOAJA. Orisa di n'elu, please make my son strong! Make his heart like a lion heart and give him eyes like an eagle!

RELATIVES. Offor!

UGBOAJA. Orisa di n'elu, please give him a heart to love and to be loved!

RELATIVES. Offor!

UGBOAJA. Orisa di n'elu (*Holding back tears.*), I know you will do these things for me. I thank you! Thank you!

(*The soft cries and whimpering of the newborn are undulating as his father lays him back on a padded bamboo bed. Family members and guests feast on boiled yam, stew, roasted corn, coconuts, and lots of palm wine.*)

Scene Five

DICK TIGER SR. Back in Oloko, Okeugo's residence was a pile of smoke. Ikonnia and the womenfolk intensified their insurrection against an imposed social anomie. On their way to the district office, a British medical officer, frightened by the protests, inadvertently runs over two women and fled on foot. The enraged women wrecked his car, chased after him, and beat him up. They proceeded to cut telegraph wires, set local courts ablaze, and blocked colonial roads. Despite police reinforcements and additional troops being called in, the women did not back down. Things got worse before they got better. When the women reached the district office, they demanded to see Captain Floyar, but their demands were met with gunshots! The gunshots dispersed the crowd but left about fifty women dead or dying. As a result of the casualties of the women's revolt, a commission was set up by the colonial administration to investigate the reasons for the uprising. Findings convinced the government to implement various administrative reforms, including the abolition of warrant chiefs and the recognition of women in the native courts. The findings also prompted the colonial administration to defer their plans to impose a tax levy on the market women.

This revolt against the colonial administration, termed the "Women's War," is the first major challenge to British authority in Nigeria and West Africa during the colonial period, and its ramifications are iconic of the role of women in the sociopolitical affairs of Nigeria and Africa today.

CHINAKA. Ewooh! *(Questioning)* Lesson? Do not anger women! There's no way you know how far they fit go to fight you back!

GODWIN. True! Those women were great. They sacrifice a lot for their families, and children's children.

GOLDSMITH. I've heard so many horrendous stories about how those warrant chiefs misbehaved towards our people.

NELSON., *adding.* To please Oyibo, right? Those liar chiefs were very wicked and deserve whatever they got from the tuff womens!

GOLDSMITH, *continuing.* About three decades later, Richard (Dick Tiger) Ihetu, born in the same year as when the women of valor fought, would fight a similar battle of historic proportions, in pursuit of dignity and honor for his people in global sports and later in the political sphere. How will Dick Tiger stand in the face of adversities? How would he handle the multiple challenges that will confront him? Will he cower and cave in? Or will he mount a battle shield and remain resolute, like the mothers of the 1929 Women's War who made a lot of sacrifices in pursuit of justice and equity for their families and generations to come? Decades later, just like the brave women fought in unity against a common irritant, Nigerians will stand in unity, despite insurmountable odds, to host a world championship fight for the first time on African soil.

DICK TIGER SR. Thank you Gordy. *(Sulking)* Now, brothers, this is the part that we may not like so much, but the truth has to be told. It's about our early years with Taatu, after the death of our father, Ugboaja.

GOLDSMITH. Is it okay that I listen to this family story with you all?

CHORUS. Sure!

CHINAKA. It is our truths. It's not a secret or embarrass to us. We thank Orisa that we survive to tell the story.

CHORUS. Hallelujah!

DICK TIGER SR. You are quite welcome to stay, Gordy. You are even going to help me with the story as we progress. You were at the fight in Ibadan, right?

GOLDSMITH. Sure. I was actually in Ibadan three days before your fight with Fullmer on August 10.

DICK TIGER SR. Yes. So, you will help me relay some part of the showdown! *(Halting)* I will also call my wife, Aby, to help me retell parts of the odyssey as we go along. My brothers Chinaka, Nelson, and Godwin will remind us any parts that we miss, because they retain intricate details better than I do. *(Smiles)* Is that okay?

GOLDSMITH. Sounds very good.

CHINAKA and GODWIN. Eyiooh!

Nelson. Let's go!

CHINAKA. First, we'll visit again things that happen in our childhood.

Act Two

SCENE ONE

DICK TIGER SR. Barely fourteen years after the women's rebellion, when Ugboaja held me, his son Richard, to the heavens, he passed on to his ancestors in the great beyond. Ejiatu was now left to cater to her four teenaged boys. Widowed and poor, her problems were compounded when her husband's kin, our uncle, Umeze Nnogbuo, hatched a devious plot against her, in the guise of upholding communal ordinances. His bone of contention—a breadfruit tree.

(*Umeze is sitting alone under the shade of a breadfruit tree overlooking his hut. He bears a very intimidating presence—deep plum-skinned, tall, heavyset with piercing red eyes and a deafening, shrill voice. Sporting a look of melancholy, he suddenly shoots up, resting large hands on his large hips.*)

UMEZE, *pacing.* (*Speaks in broken English*) For many, many years since, this tree *(Pointing to a breadfruit tree.)* never bore any fruits! And with all its green, wavy, leaves! (*Crestfallen*) But, Ugboaja's family—they can carry buckets and buckets of nutrient breadfruits from their breadfruit tree to the market (*Mumbles*) making money! A lot money from the tree's big (*Demonstrating*), big breadfruits! (*Maliciously*) I nu kwa!

Imagine that! *(Pause)* Well, *(Shifting his big red eyes side to side.)* well, Ugboaja is no mooh! He die. Now that he gone, *(Emphatically)* I must to cut down that demon tree that have bewitched my own tree! *(Adjusting his wrap, pushing out his lips.)* Mmhu! Ejiatu must be put to her place. *(Stressing)* She be a common widow and poor! *(Pause)* I dey warn her long, long time to down that wild tree that always shooting big, big breadfruits on the busy pathway! *(Incredulously)* Those breadfruit lumps fit be deadly as bullet shells in a riffle, and, and fit easily smash person to die! *(Wryly)* I no go allow Ejiatu have that tree! *(Frantically undoing and retying his wrap, pushing out his chest.)* Besides, I'll be doing all of our peoples in Eluowerre community a big favor *(Demonstrating)*, because the biggest of the big, big breadfruit lumps can fall and hurt, or even kill any of all of us wey dey walk pass that pathway! *(Beating his chest)* I, Umeze, no go sit here and allow it! *(Hastily exits.)*

SCENE TWO

DICK TIGER SR. A beaten path stretches from Ejiatu's residence through an alley to Umeze's compound. There are many trees and plants lining the unpaved roads. Next to the alley is Ejiatu's garden where at the center of a busy pathway lies a towering breadfruit tree she inherited from her late husband. The tree had over the years proved a valuable food source and cash crop for Ejiatu and her family. About sixty feet tall, its branches are covered in deep green, lobed leaves from which dangle luscious green globes of breadfruit, each weighing up to ten pounds. The breadfruit tree is the crux of the matter when Umeze reaches Ejiatu's residence. He quickly draws her into a contentious argument that ultimately shatters her simple life and momentarily thrusts her into a world of grief and uncertainties.

(Tending to some crops in her garden, Ejiatu dons a cotton wrap around her body, dripping down to her knees. Sweating profusely, her singing

belies the decapitating effects of the sweltering heat. Called Taatu, Ejiatu is a slim, freckle-faced, middle-aged woman, about five feet, seven inches tall. She has caramel-colored skin and striking features that seem worn by years of toiling. She, like Umeze, also speaks pidgin, or broken English.)

EJIATU., *singing.* Chineke anyi i di mma, eehh! Idi nma, Chukwu kere uwa i di mma, oge nile! (x2)

(*Translation: Our God You are good. Yes, you are good. Creator of heaven and earth You are good, all the time!*)

(*Umeze, approaching Ejiatu's residence can hear her cheerful singing, and he is repulsed.*)

UMEZE., *shrieking.* Ejiatu! Ejiatu!

(*Ejiatu abruptly stops singing. She knows that voice, and though tense with fear, she puts up a good front.*)

EJIATU., *smiling.* Ewoo, De'm Umeze, anwula oo (Greetings). You are welcome. *(Fidgeting)* I fit get you cup of cold water?

UMEZE., *dismissively.* Forget that, Ejiatu! How many times have I ask you to cut down that breadfruit tree? Its big, big lumps may soon fall on somebody. You dey wait for when one of the lumps finally fall on one or two of our peoples to die? *(Pause)* I tell you long time before to cut that tree. Then the other day, I send Oguzie, our village clerk, to tell you to cut down that tree! You no listen. Last week, I ask Cornelius, the town crier, to deliver same message again. *(Pointing at Ejiatu.)* Have you cuts down the tree? *(Pauses)* No! *(Livid)* Its leaves are continue flapping and dancing wickedly in the wind!

EJIATU., *with lips trembling.* Nna anyi (Our uncle), biko (Please), it won't not fall and kill nobody. Truth. It been there since I marry your broda, Ihetu Ugboaja, and it never fall on nobody and won't, never. Please, I (*Mumbles*) cannot cut—

UMEZE., *interrupting*. Why you obey not me! Hah? Even when am tell you so many times? (*Shouting*) You must do as I said!

EJIATU., *feeling a lump in her throat; tears welling in her eyes*. Nna anyi, you broda, Ugboaja leave that breadfruit tree to his first sons, Chinaka (*Hands outstretched, pleading*) Please, that na all we have, and Ugboaja, your broda (*mumbles*) my husband, go dey turn in him grave if he know it be cut down.

UMEZE, *impatiently*. Nwanyi, shut up! Ugboaja won't want breadfruit fall to kill anybody. Truth? (*Rolling fiery red eyes*) Now, bring peoples to quick-quick cut that accurse tree down! (*Shaking his head, ostensibly*) I can't not let it kill any of my brodas or sistas in dis village. (*Sternly*) It must go down! (*He begins to leave.*)

EJIATU., *quickly kneeling in front of him*. Ewuu! De'm Umeze, biko, please leave that tree for we and my chidrens. It is all them papa leave them. Please.

UMEZE, *shoving her to the ground*. You must, will do as I said, or I go cut the witch tree down myself! (*He continues to exit.*)

(*Humiliated, but buoyed by determination, Ejiatu shoots up and musters all her strength to push back.*)

EJIATU, *calling out to him*. Leaves we alone! What we do you? (*Frustrated*) De Umeze Nnogbuo! Why you wicked we? Leave we, my childrens alone!

UMEZE, *twisting his face to a scowl, eyes like red lightening, turns back to Ejiatu*. How dare you talk with me like that! You go pay for this, Ejiatu! You be but a womans! We pay dowry on your head! *(Ejiatu manages a brave smile.)* So, you must, because of that, do as I said! *(He storms off.)*

EJIATU, *though beaten, remains resolute, calling out to him, again.* Leave we, my childrens alone! *(Louder and stronger)* De Umeze Nnogbuo, Leave we, my chidrens alone!

(Mindful of Umeze's sphere of influence in the village, Ejiatu is distressed, as her eyes search the skies. Her hands vigorously shaking she blurts out)

Ukwu jie agu! Ukwu jie agu, ngbada a bia ya ugwo! *(Pause)* Ukwu jie agu, mgbada a bia ya ugwo! (When a lion is wounded, he's vulnerable and prey to smaller animals!) Ewuu u! *(Pause)* Ihetu Ugboaja, di'm! (My husband!) Why you leave we, my childrens so soon? Ewuu u! *(Still in shock, shaking her head incredulously, exits.)*

SCENE THREE

DICK TIGER SR. About a week after Ejiatu's encounter with Umeze, four strange men encroached upon her garden on a balmy afternoon to carry out Umeze's devious orders. Oblivious of her ongoing confrontations with Umeze, the villagers watch helplessly in shock as the towering breadfruit tree, with the oscillating moves, was woefully thrashed by some unknown assailants. The men painstakingly downed the giant breadfruit tree, cut it into huge chunks, stacking it miles high with careless abandon in the center of a busy pathway.

(A loud bang forces Ejiatu and some of the villagers out of their huts and unto the scene of the commotion.)

EJIATU, *rushing to the site, clutching her chest.* Ewoo! Ewuu! *(Incoherent)* My help...my big...big help breafru...tree! Ahhrrr!

(Bewildered) Why? Why?

(The villagers gather to console her.)

EJIATU, *shouting.* Umeze Nnogbuo! Why? *(With hands outstretched, eyes searching the sky.)* I hu kwa la, Amaigbo? (Amaigbo, you seeing this?) *(Sobbing)* Ishi Igbo! Amaigbo nwe'm nu, I hu kwala! (My great hometown of Amaigbo, do you see what's happening here?) Orisa di n elu, I hu kwa la! (God in heaven, bear me witness!) *(Looking to the heavens, shrieks)* Kpee nna! Orisa Kpee! O gi nwe ikpe! (God in heaven, judge! You are the greatest Judge! Judge Umeze Nnogbuo!)

(As she struggles to compose herself, some villagers visibly moved by her plight proceed to escort her back to her hut, with her teenage boys in tow. A few days later, Ejiatu, fearing retribution from village folks about the downed tree's obstruction of the busy pathway, subsequently hires help to cart chunks of the tree to the market.)

SCENE FOUR

DICK TIGER SR. Ejiatu, our mother, suffered other losses precluding the loss of her valuable breadfruit tree. The losses unleashed undue emotional and financial strains on our family. Unable to adequately care for her boys after years of struggling alone, without support or consideration from her late husband's next of kin, Ejiatu is forced to leave her matrimonial home. She and her children move into her father's compound in Umuchoke, Amaigbo, at the invitation of her only brother, Ezeabasirim Ononiwu. After many years living with our uncle, Ezeabasirim, there came time for my brothers and I to leave, to venture out into the world. Ejiatu braces for that decision that will shake the very structure of her family. Before the break of dawn, she wakes us up for a family meeting.

EJIATU, *summoning her children*. Come, my sons *(Pause)* Chinaka! Nelson! Diki! Godwin! Unu bia! (Y'all come!)

(The screeching of roosters can be heard signaling the dawn of a new day. The winning chatter of birds and the bleating of goats disrupt the dead silence of night in the village of Amaigbo. Ezeabasirim Ononiwu's residence is just one of the very modest mixes of sand and clay huts scattered throughout the village. The roof, like those of most of the huts in the area, is made of rusty, patched corrugated metal. There are three rooms inside the hut. Each room has a small window that is separated by colored or dyed raffia mats. A clay water pot sits on a side of the living room. The pot has a cover and on top of it sit two calabash drinking cups. There's a flickering of light from a smoky oil lantern sitting in the center of the room. As she calls, each of her sons stirs and like clockwork, begins to roll up his sleeping mat. They all speak in broken English.)

CHINAKA, *rubbing his eyes*. Taatu, wetin happen? Everything okay?

(Chinaka, the oldest and closest to his mother, considers himself the family sentry, who watches over the household. He is slim and introverted, but can be outspoken when occasion warrants. As they gather, he senses that all is not well.)

EJIATU, *sorrowfully*. Times be very tough for we now. Since your papa die, things hard for me to keep up with the chicken farming. Most the chickens die all during chicken sickness, and I no afford feed for the ones living. Farm products no bringin' money, no mooh sweet, big breadfruit *(Pauses; sighs)*, and it be a lot hard *(Pause)* lot hard to make it well. *(She slowly walks up to the water pot, scoops some water, and gulps.)* I no fit be able pay school fees for all you. *(Choking back tears, she speaks softly.)* My broda, Ezeabasirim, also try a lot. I go send all you to city where you uncles fit help una learn trade, so that one day, you fit begin you own businesses.

NELSON, *unperturbed*. Which uncle you go send us to *sef*? (Anyway?)

GODWIN. We never leave village befo. How we go survive city?

(*Nelson is the shortest and wittiest of his siblings. He is wiry and has a raspy voice, which he never fails to crank up to drive his point home. Godwin, though the youngest, is the tallest. He's easygoing and responsible.*)

(*Jovial, but reserved, Richard called Diki by friends and family members, exudes a quiet confidence. He has a stocky, athletic physique, and when he smiles, which is often, a set of pearly white teeth sharply contrasts with his richly dark complexion.*)

DIKI. You go be okay, Taatu? How you go manage to do?

EJIATU, *voice subdued*. Uh (*Pause*) make una no worry about me. I go manage whatever crops I fit grow from we garden here in village. (*Pause*) You be good boys, oo! Remember always to work hard and (*She pulls on her ears; while focusing her gaze on them, stresses her next command.*) Pray! Pray! Pray! Remember (*Pause*) no suffering is permanent with God!

CHINAKA, *pouting*. Well, I no go-go city! (*Pauses*) The village na my only home. I no think say I fit survive city life, and I know some of them uncles. (*He smiles maliciously.*) Them no good!

NELSON. At least we go be able eat two times a day, and learn trading.

GODWIN. We will miss you, Taatu. We will also miss uncle Ezeabasirim.

DIKI. Who we go stay with anyway?

EJIATU. You, Diki, you go live with you Uncle Iwenta in Enugu. He go teach you to be carpenter. Nelson and Godwin, you go stay with una Uncle Ndubaku in Aba. He get small store and him go teach you how to buying and selling for Ekeoha Market in Aba.

DIKI, *sadly*. Oh, but why I have to go by myself? I go be missing everybody.

CHINAKA, *mockingly*. You be the strongest and a lonely child. Ha! Ha! Nobody want you!

EJIATU, *to Dick*. No mind him. (*To all*) Chinaka go be the lonely one to stay here in village all by himself, with him ol' mama and fewer chickins! (*They chuckle.*) Diki go go Enugu by himsef, because I know he strong. (*She laughs softly.*) Yes, Orisa di n'elu build my son so, so strong, and I trusting that he fight for himsef any place, any times. *(Pausing)* Now, I will give una each a small help. (*She reaches into her bosom and pulls out a knotted handkerchief. Carefully unties it, takes out a small bunch of coins, and with hands trembling, gives one coin each to her departing sons.)* This is all am have left. Use it to go una uncle houses safe. (*Struggles to control her emotions.*) Now come. (*She kneels.*) Make we pray. (*The others kneel; she leads the prayer.*)

Scene Five

DICK TIGER SR. While at Enugu, things did not go as planned for me. I was relegated to performing mere household chores and subjected to tremendous physical and verbal abuse by my uncle, Iwenta. I hastily planned a daring escape.

(*At his uncle's house in Enugu, Dick, alone, ponders his fate.*)

DIKI, *distraught*. Oh, God! Wetin I dey do here sef? (*Pause*) Taatu tell me I go be learning trade here with Uncle Iwenta, but he lies. He lies! (*He puts both hands on his head.*) Wetin am going to do? (*Pause*) I no have money to go back to village or move to Aba. I dey here for months now, no work. (*Horrified*) Me no fit live like this for all my life! (*He paces restlessly.*) Him feed me small, small food and whip me every hour on the hour (Pauses) Why he treat me so? (*He kicks his feet and punches the air.*) I tell him I'll be bigger than him one day, but he laugh and kick me around like football. (*Suddenly he brightens up.*) I got it! Yes! Yes! I will run. I run, run away! (*He frantically throws his belongings into a knapsack.*) I go go to the railway station, and I go hop, skip from train to train between stations until I get to Aba! (*He throws the knapsack onto his back.*) Make I hurry quick and get out befo' them return. (*He leaves.*)

SCENE SIX

DICK TIGER SR. I couldn't wait to leave my uncle's house and never to return. I was able to stow away in a train and change trains at each stop all the way from Enugu City to another city, Aba. I reunited with Godwin and Nelson who sadly report that under the guardianship of our uncle Ndubaku, they too suffered the same fate as I. My brothers and I decided that it is time to branch out on our own.

(*The three brothers reunite at a street corner in Aba.*)

DIKI, *approaching his brothers smiles warmly*. It's good to see you all again!

GODWIN, *looking him up and down*. Diki, you lose a lot of weight.

NELSON, *examining each of his brothers and himself.* It look like we all lose a lot of weight. (*Pause.*) Diki, how was things for you at Uncle Iwenta?

DIKI. It was bad, bad! (*He shrugs his shoulders in disgust.*) Na big waste of my time be that!

NELSON. Did he beat you with broom, too?

DIKI. No, worse. He use sticks beat me, and he no let me even see him workshop (*mumbles*) he say that I go be better working as a cook and cleaner. (*Exclaiming*) Tuffiakwa! (Horrific!)

GODWIN, *amazed.* Some of these uncles dey very, very wicked o!

DIKI. Eyii! Chinaka was right! They're—(*Like in a trance, his eyes suddenly become fixed on a magazine cover.*)

NELSON. He make you mop floors five times a day? (*He notices Dick's gaze and yells.*) Well, Diki! He make you mop floors?

DIKI, *startled.* Uh…oh, I just dey look the boxing magazines. (*Quickly*) I think I want become boxer! (*Pointing as he strikes a boxing pose.*) Look, look at them boxers! Them look powerful!

NELSON, *confused.* Huh? (*Ignoring Dick's last comment*) Okay (mumbles) Diki, make we go find way to make money fast, or we all go starve for hunger. (*Begins to leave with Godwin.*) C'mon.

DIKI, *abruptly.* Wait, I get idea. (*Speaking slowly*) We go go round and pick empty bottles and cans and change them for money at the brewery; that way, we fit feed ourself and help put a roof over we head.

GODWIN, *bewildered.* You mean we fit make money selling old bottle and container? How is that?

DIKI. Yes. We go go round pickin' all empty bottle and can, then we go carry them to brewery in town and get small money from them. The brewery clean the cans and use them again in their businesses. (*He throws both hands up.*) It's either that, or we go starve nah. (*His eyes glisten.*) Then I go fit have time learn to box!

NELSON. That sound good. (*He wrinkles his face.*) But, Diki, who tell you say you fit make it as boxer sef? You know boxers always dey in gym, training a lot much hard to win an—

GODWIN, *interjecting.* And to make sure say no one beat them up or knock them out! (*Pause*) That boxing thing be one danger sport, Diki. You no want make them hurt you. Remember Taatu—

DIKI, *boldly.* I no go get hurt, and I no go get knock out. I defend myself *(pause)* and I go be knocking others out in the ring for the future! (*Quickly*) You know, I fit become...world champion!

NELSON, *laughing hysterically with Godwin.* Oh, okay! (*Mockingly*) Black Bomber! (*Snickering*) Please, make we get out there pick some bottles...Make we no starve.

DIKI, *assuredly.* I go be world champion, and *(mumbles)* I go travel all the world, for sure!

GODWIN, *eyeing Dick cautiously.* Come, make we go. We need pick bottle to feed, and pay for small rent. I don tire to dey sleep outside for people corridor.

SCENE SEVEN

DICK TIGER SR. I grew increasingly interested in boxing, and by the late 1940s, I had struck up a solid friendship with Gordy "Goldsmith." We set up a boxing club together, gathering up neighborhood and street kids interested in boxing. We thumbed through lots of boxing magazines, observing the boxers poses, and watched cinema presentations of American fights to gain some boxing knowledge and inspiration. I am inspired by the great boxers I watched and read about. After weeks of hard work recycling bottles, my brothers and I are able to rent a tiny cubicle. I used some of my meager earnings to pay for boxing lessons at the Emy Boxing Club.

(*At the Emy Boxing Club, fighters and would-be fighters mill around the cramped space. Boxing equipment and gear are few and worn from overuse. Dick enters the club with his brothers.*)

DIKI. This is where I come for boxing lessons. After the lessons, Gordy Goldsmith and I go to the boxing club that we started.

NELSON, *shocked.* You started a boxing club? With the small money we make from bottle pickin', how you able pay for the classes? Gordy pay too?

GODWIN. Eyii, how una manage to dey pay?

DIKI. Well, we don dey do much better now for our bottle business. I come only three times a week, but I help with maintenance in the gym, me and Gordy. So, we dey only pay for the first lesson in a week.

GODWIN. That na good plan, Diki. It be like say you dey enjoy this boxing thin' a lot.

DIKI. Yes. I dey also watch American fighters on film, and from there I do learn some more boxing movements. (*Excitedly striking boxing poses; air-boxing.*) Mr. Gikonuo, the manager, even say he go soon sign me up to fight the amateurs!

NELSON, *gasps.* I hear from Chinaka yesterday.

DIKI, *concerned.* Wetin he talk? Is Taatu okay?

NELSON, *clears his throat.* Chinaka say that somehow Taatu learn say you want start this boxing business seriously. She dey very sad about it and dey fear say you go hurt yoursef in the fights. She get the support of the whole village on this concern. (*Pauses*) Diki, them all dey fear say you go break Taatu's heart. (*pause*) She's already a poor widow! Them say you fit get your jaws broke, or even be killed in the boxing ring …No one from our village ever try to do this so much danger sport, boxing. (*Speaking slowly, deliberately.*) Taatu want make you stop this boxin' thin'. Everybody for inside village say you must please learn a trade, or any other work wey no be boxing.

DIKI, *sternly.* You know that I no fit stop boxin' now. I get strong love for the sport! I no fit give it up now, please. (*Pause*) Besides, our father, Ihetu Ugboaja, and his father before him, be well popular wrestlers! (*Quickly*) If you ask me, wrestling be just as danger as boxing (*mumbles*) and football! (*Pause*) Haven't you see young mens carried out of a football match on a stretching table? Some get them legs broke for the rest of they lives! (*Desperately*) Look, the amateur divisions will soon pay me small money, and with money from we bottle business, I fit go night school for increase in my education. (*pauses*) Just promise me, Nelson, and Godwin that you no go ask, and no go tell Taatu any more news about my boxing business plans. Okay? Please. (*Pause*) We no go ever again dey poor. Not ever, by power of God.

GODWIN. Amin! Oh, God, please help us! (*Shaking his head in amazement.*) Diki have always been sure of himsef. (*To Nelson*) Remember? Whenever we dey out dey pick bottle, (*Demonstrating*) Diki dey always dey gentleman…even when people dey try make him mad. Some of them even jeer him and tease, asking', "Why you a common bottle picker like to dey carry yoursef with such airs as if you be the rich and famous? Who you think you be sef?"

DIKI, *unruffled.* But na them dey bring us the bottles and containers wey we dey sell. If I go get down them level and insult them back, then them no go want give us any bottle, no containers to sell to brewery. No be so? (*Quickly*) Na so. Them be like we customer, so make we be good to them always.

GODWIN, *incredulously.* Even when them dey so wicked to you? Nooh! I no think I mysef fit take them rubbi—

DIKI, *interrupting.* That na how things go be, if we are going to collect enough bottles to sell. We need to eat (*mumbles*) and so does Taatu. (*Smirking*) But, you know (*mumbles*) If them try make me mad outside of work, I go push back in full force! (*Smiling broadly.*) Anyways, it no matter wetin them say or think. I know say everybody go know me one day, and I know say I go marry a be-au-ti-ful wife, and travel abroad to ala ndi ocha (Europe and America) (*He and Godwin laugh*), where I go become rich and famous!

NELSON, *unamused.* Well, look oo…as long as your boxing work no dey hurt our bottle-pickin' business. (*Wryly.*) 'Cause right now, this boxing dream of yours be just that—a dream, like chasing shadow. (*Pause.*) One bird in hand dey worth more than one dozen of them in the bush!

DIKI., *slightly subdued.* I understand, Nelson. Believe me, I do, and I tell you now that I no go waste my time, or yours. (*Pause)* Just be small patient with me.

SCENE EIGHT

DICK TIGER SR. By the early 1950s, I had built an impressive fight record. Over a two-year period as an amateur, I won thirty out of thirty-two fights. I also took on the stage pseudonym, "Dick Tiger," and it was by this time that I seriously considered boxing as a lifetime career.

(*The brothers are scavenging for empty bottles and cans littered in a football field in Aba.*)

NELSON, *playfully.* Godwin, have you heard? Diki dey now go by the name, Dick Tiger!

GODWIN. Yes, that's a good show name.

DICK TIGER. But do you know why I wanted that name?

NELSON, *credulously.* Well, everybody knows say that (*pauses)* it must be 'cause you (mumbling) trap and jump on your opponent, like a tiger!

GODWIN, *affirmatively.* Oh, yes! (*Demonstrating)* Diki, just dey keep tracking the other fighter until he (mumbling) catches am and begins to dey rain punch for am! (*They laugh.*)

DICK TIGER. You are both right. Me, I like the name…it fit my style. (*Pause.*) Look oo, I think say I want make this boxing work my work for life. I think say I fit make much more money for all of us.

GODWIN, *cautiously.* I don't know how Taatu go feel about that o.

DICK TIGER. She go feel good about it soon. (*He winks.*) She go get use to better quality life *(Smiling mischievously),* how she no go like am?

GODWIN. (*There's silence as each looks at the others.*) We go all get use to better quality life. May Orisa be your guide and help us all.

NELSON and DICK. Amen oo!

Scene Nine

DICK TIGER SR. In 1952, I turned professional, and Jack Farnsworth, a British boxing official, recommended me to the Nigerian Boxing Board of Control (NBBC) in Lagos. Within three years of turning pro, I was able to win national laurels. As a result of my wins in boxing, Farnsworth sent me off to Liverpool, England, under the management of Peter Banasko, who was subsequently replaced by Tony Vairo. However, I did not find it easy to cope with all the changes in my new life in Britain. I seriously wondered whether the adverse conditions I was experiencing would derail my chances of making it in the big fights.

(The gym in Liverpool is a crowded, drab space. Jump ropes hang loosely on the only boxing ring, and speed and heavy bags hang adjacent to each other in the cloistered environment. Vairo, a veteran in the boxing business and a shrewd negotiator, confronts Tiger.)

VAIRO, *upset.* Dick, you really need to work harder in order to win fights. (*Sternly*) You are strong enough! We are going to put you through more rigorous training rituals, so that you can acquire better boxing skills to make some wins! (*Pauses)* Your punches are careless, and your boxing stance is lousy. *(Motioning to Tiger, he abruptly spreads his legs apart, holds his fists up almost covering his eyes, and casually drags his feet to mimic Tiger's movements in the ring.)* You do not have the essentials of foot-and-hand speed! That is why the crafty boxers that are quick-footed and sharp are able to gauge when to move in to land a stinging punch to destabilize you. *(Demonstrating)* They consistently reach and jab, reach and jab, and move away from your lead feet as quickly as they came! (*Threatening*) If you keep losing fights, you will have to look for another manager!

DICK TIGER., *apologetically.* Err *(mumbles)* oh, alright, Mr. Vairo. I am sorry. (*Timidly*) I am thankful for the job you got me at the paint factory. *(Reluctantly)* It's just that after putting in long hours working there and without a good diet, I am very tired and unable to focus during training. After a day's work at the factory, I usually feel dizzy and very tired, too tired even to walk home *(mumbles)* let alone work out.

VAIRO, *casually.* Really? Well, I hope you keep your nose covered. (*He points at Dick's face.*) The fumes from the paint mixes can be toxic, meaning, it can bloody kill you. (*He places both hands in his pockets.*) Anyway, we will intensify your workouts. You will have to improve your skills, Tiger. You are strong enough and have great potentials of becoming Britain's middleweight boxing champion or world boxing champion. Also, try your best to get used to the food here. It's not so bad! (*He storms off.*)

TIGER., *alone and frustrated.* In Nigeria, you become a champion because you are strong and aggressive enough to beat down the other fighter. But over here, they praise "fancy boxers" and how well you can dodge and run away from their opponent in the ring! (*He sighs.*) I did not train to be a runner! (*Putting his hands over his forehead.*) I've now lost four fights in a row since coming into this country. (*Bewildered*) How can that be? Each time my opponents are given a decision win over me! (*He straightens himself.*) Yes, I am a strong and aggressive fighter, and if I'm going to become international champion, I better work hard to win (*pauses*) by scoring total knockouts! (*Pause*) I can no longer afford to leave my fate in the hands of the British judges! (*Feeling dizzy, he sits.*) And if I'm going to become champion—world champion, I better first leave the job at the paint factory. (*Shaking his head in confirmation*) I get too tired and weak after working in there. (*Quickly*) I'll see if there's an opening at the lumber yard. Also (*feeling encouraged*), if I am going to be champion, I must improve my diet! It's been tough for me to adjust to the types of food served here—sausage, eggs, mashed potato, gravy. (*Quickly*) I'll telegram Godwin for some wholesome African food.

(*Suddenly, feeling a bit depressed.*) I am so lonely, not even the best cooking in the world could quite wean me from the loneliness that's gripped me lately! (*Clutching his heart.*) I need a life partner—a wife (*mumbles*) to love and to reassure me that things will be all right. (*Pause.*) I will ask my brothers to help me find my beau-ti-ful wife! (*He struggles to laugh, then finds a sheet of paper and begins to write.*)

Act Three

SCENE ONE

DICK TIGER SR. Godwin read a telegram he just received from me. I sounded desperate, and Godwin was deeply moved, and proceeded to rally my other siblings to get me the much-needed help I crave.

(*In Aba, Nelson has married his sweetheart, Christiana, and moved out. So, Godwin is now the sole occupant of the tiny cubicle they once shared. Sitting on a kitchen stool over a flickering kerosene lantern, he reads a telegrammed message from Dick Tiger.*)

GODWIN., *reading.*

Goddy nwanne'm,

life here rough. I starve. Europe foods make stomach turn and need control bowels for training. Send okporoko, egusi, achi, dried pepper, garri, crayfish, and other things for good soup! Need real Africa food to get power back. I need win fights, or manager, Vairo, send me packing. Please, also I need you and brothers to help me find my wife, please. I very lonely. Greet everybody, specially, Mama Ejiatu. Don't tell am suffering over here. Things will be all right.

Your broda, Diki.

(*Folding telegram, sadly*) Oh, my dear brother! We go do everything we fit to make sure all things are good for you. (*Pause.*) I go go go meet Nelson and Chinaka; we go bring money together get the food things. We go also decide best way to find you your beau-ti-ful wife! (*Smiling warmly, exits.*).

Scene Two

DICK TIGER SR. As with most African customs, especially in these times, the responsibility of finding a life partner usually falls on the male members in the immediate family. So, my brothers, Chinaka, Nelson, and Godwin embark on a mission to find me my beautiful bride.

GODWIN, *to Nelson and Chinaka*. What news from Matilda family since? It been most six weeks since we went to they family compound for the first introductions.

CHINAKA, *waving his hands*. Oh, please no mind them. Her mother specially was very crazy and hard. (*He is visibly upset.*) Can you believe what she say?

NELSON and GODWIN., *anxiously*. What?

CHINAKA, She said she don't want her daughter marry Diki 'cause he be in job where people get beatings and hurt, and she is afraid that her daughter be getting beats and patches in body if she marry Diki. (*contemptuous*)Imagine that!

GODWIN, *slightly amused*. How foolish!

NELSON, *contemptuously*. Oh please, let's leave them to continue in their village life!

CHINAKA. Yes! The mother said that her daughter is already been promise to marry the chief of another village. She say she rather Matilda marry a chief, so she can become queen mother of the bride.

NELSON., *tickled*. Queen mother indeed! (*Sarcastically*.) No, she will even become Queen Elizabeth of Igbo nile, gburugburu! (Of Igbo people world-wide!) (*They all laugh*.) Nonsense!

GODWIN. Make we forget them. (*To Chinaka*.) Last week, you say you were going to talk to your good teacher friend in the village of Orlu about this matter. Did you?

CHINAKA, *brightening*. Yes, (*Pauses*) I talk to Asiegbu. I explain that Diki is our brother looking for a good wife to join him in England where he training hard to become world champion.

NELSON and GODWIN, *anxiously*. Ahaaa?

NELSON. Wetin he say?

CHINAKA, *amused*. He be more interested in talking about Diki and boxing, but when he see my serious look to find a good mate for our brother, he be more serious to cooperate. He tell me that at the teacher college, in Amaumara, is a beautiful young lady name, Abigail Ogbuji, who he say is very good with caring, know a lot of very good things, and respect everybody. She from village of Amike, in Orlu.

GODWIN. Have you see her yet?

CHINAKA. No, but he tell me that she be very beautiful inside and out. A lot of mens he say come to marry her, but she want to finish teacher school first, so that she fit help her mama and papa, Chief and Mrs. Jacob Ogbuji, to help her family.

NELSON, *relieved.* This sound like she be good wife for Diki. (*He looks around, seeking agreement.*) We know Diki no need crazy in his life at all. He just want work hard to win, and this Abigail lady is like just what Orisa want for Diki!

GODWIN. Eyiioo! (Yes!) I hope say she not already promise to marry any other man yet. Please, let rush to Amike,

CHINAKA. Now that we agree say Abigail sound like a good wife for Diki, I will ask my friend to bring us to her family. (*Pause.*) It is well.

GODWIN and NELSON. Eyiioo. (In agreement) It is well. (*They exit.*).

SCENE THREE

DICK TIGER SR. A few months later, I received my parcel of food stuff and was able to cook some Nigerian cuisines. My strength and zeal in the fight returned full force, and I was coping better with the winter weather. I won my next four fights, even ditching the popular Terry Downes, twice at the Shoreditch Town Hall Ring in London on May 14, 1957. A year later, in Liverpool, I knocked out Pat McAteer to become the new British Empire Middleweight champion. Nigerians were jubilant over my recent triumphs in England.

(*As the city of Aba is engrossed in celebrations of Dick Tiger's win*)

GODWIN, *aside to Nelson.* Our brother, Diki Tiger, is now an international boxing champion! What some good fufu and egusi soup can do! (*Mumbles*) Belle full! (*They chuckle.*)

NELSON, *animatedly.* Eyii oo! Africa Power! Now we know he must be ready and longing for his beau-ti-ful wife!

BOTH. Eyii oo! (*Laughing, they rejoin the celebration.*)

WOMEN'S DANCE GROUP, *singing,*

Dick Tiga, nwoke oma kwuru na ya ga enwe nmeri, ekpere Nigeria eruole Chukwu nti, Dick emeriela! Umu Nigeriaaaa, were nu ya gawaaa! Ekpere Nigeria eruole Chukwu nti oo, Dick emeriela! (*x2*)

(*They whistle and the singing fades.*)

[Translation: Dick Tiger, handsome man, said that he will have victory! God has heard the prayers of Nigerians; Dick Tiger is victorious! Nigerians, let's go! Rejoice! God has heard Nigeria's prayers; Dick Tiger is victorious!) x2

SCENE FOUR

DICK TIGER SR. Sitting under the night sky with her sons in the family compound, Ejiatu expressed her gratitude to Chinaka, Nelson, and Godwin, my siblings, for their invaluable assistance in finding me a beautiful, lovely wife named, Abigail. She also expressed her delight at her sons ability to finally take the bull by the horns to return us from our maternal home to our rightful place at the Ihetu family compound in Eluowerre Ubahu, Amaigbo. There was a lot of rejoicing, and hope for a brighter future for the family.

(*A bright fire blazes in an iron cooking rack.*)

EJIATU. You young mens have fight like lions and tigers for your broda, my son (*she smiles*) Diki Tiga! You get him good wife! (*Struggling to control her emotions*) Your papa be so proud you, if he be living today.

CHINAKA, *handing her a handkerchief.* It's all right, Taatu.

EJIATU, *continuing*. You, my young mens, wipe shame from my face, and return us back to we own home, here in Eluowerre, Ubahu. (*Pauses*) God Almighty will surely bless you all for me.

CHORUS. Amen!

CHINAKA. We did what we do, as men in family. (*Smiling*) Diki send most of the money, and we move!

NELSON. I miss Uncle Ezeabasirim. He treat we well like a father.

GODWIN and CHINAKA, *chorus*. Eyiooh!

GODWIN. Uncle Ezeabasirim was good to us.

EJIATU. Yes. He be my good broda. (*Pauses*) He be good man, and God will bless him too, (*fighting off tears*) and even for take care a widow sistar and her childrens.

ALL. AMEN!

EJIATU, *wiping teardrops from her face*. I be very happy, very thank you to Orisa Almighty, for all that happen, also at meeting with Abigail family. Orisa ndewo o!

GODWIN. It was good meeting. Abigail family is good.

NELSON. Eyii, they treat us with kindest respect, and I feel very, very well with them.

CHINAKA. Eyii! I feel like that too, more than with every other family we visited in lookin' for Diki's good wife.

EJIATU, *looks up to the heavens, smiling from ear to ear*. Orisa di n'elu thank you oo!

Abigail, in London. Circa 1958.

SCENE FIVE

DICK TIGER SR. While in England, my boxing skills continued to peak. I was able to demolish my opponents in the British roped ring and had my sights set on America, especially on Madison Square Garden, considered to be the "bleeding edge of boxing." Though cognizant of the fact that winning laurels in America would pave the way for me to compete in the world boxing championships league, I also knew that I would need the direction of a skilled manager, and I believed I found that in Mr. Wilfred "Jersey" Jones. Before I could transition however, I needed to settle scores with my current manager, Mr. Tony Vairo. After all's said and done, I proceeded to my homeland of Nigeria to bring my new bride to England. Loneliness was now alien to me, and within months we left the shores of England to America.

(*In Liverpool, Tiger is speaking with his manager, Vairo.*)

DICK TIGER, *in his blunt form.* I think that I should venture into American boxing. I want to leave England to travel to America.

VAIRO, *shocked.* But (*mumbles*) Dick (*Pause*) You are doing so well here in Liverpool. You've already won four fights in a row— by knockouts! You even stopped the great Pat McAteer to become the British Empire Middleweight Boxing Champion! *(Speaks slowly, deliberately.)* Leaving Liverpool could mess things up for you and your new wife.

DICK TIGER, *thoughtfully.* I understand, Mr. Vairo. No one is sure what the future holds. *(Pause)* I will move to America, where I will have the opportunity to duel with some of the best fighters in the sport.

VAIRO. Yes, they have some of the best in the world, but who is going to manage you over there? (*Growing agitated*) Do you have a skilled hand to help you elevate your fight game to where you desire it? To world championship levels? (*Pauses*) Hah?

DICK TIGER. Yes. His name is Wilfred "Jersey" Jones. He is a seasoned manager, who has groomed the likes of Hogan Bassey and a host of other professional fighters to become world champions in their divisions.

VAIRO, *looking away.* Hogan referred you?

DICK TIGER. Jersey's name had come up in our conversations since I started contemplating world rankings. I've seen his work portfolio, and it is impressive, so I figured I give him a shot at managing my career when I make the move to America.

VAIRO, *hesitantly*. Very well. (*Straightening himself*) If that is what you want, I know that I cannot persuade you otherwise.

DICK TIGER. While I hold dear my current title as the British Empire Middleweight Champion, I want to become the middleweight champion of the whole world. *(Tenderly)* Mr. Vairo, I know that it is not due to a lack of effort on your part that you haven't found me a suitable opposition, but I have a searing ambition stirring in me to break into the world rankings; therefore, I must go to America, if I am to become world champion. There, I will have the opportunity to be matched with some of the best in boxing.

VAIRO. Good luck, Champion! *(Shaking Tiger's hands)* Best wishes to you and your lovely wife, Abigail.

DICK TIGER. I remain indebted for all you have taught me about the fight game. (*Smiles*) Thank you very much, my friend. Good luck to you too.

Act Four

Scene One

ABIGAIL. My husband, Dick Tiger, and I settled in New York City in early 1959. We found America's weather more agreeable than England's. However, after a few years, with our twins, another daughter, and a fourth child on the way, my husband and I needed a readjustment in our family structure.

(*In their moderately furnished suite at the Colonial Hotel in New York City.*)

ABIGAIL, *AT the dinner table; momentarily glancing at Dick's plate.* Di'm, you are such a good sport. You have totally immersed yourself in the Western culture now—

DICK TIGER, *jokingly.* Woman! Are you now calling me black oyibo, because I was able to finish a plate of spaghetti?

ABIGAIL, *mischievously.* No! You are too black to be oyibo. (*Giggling*) It's because I don't think that I've ever seen you attack a plate of non-African cuisine with such ferocity!

(*They laugh.*)

DICK TIGER, *affectionately*. Aby, you seem much happier here in the USA. It isn't as cold here, I've noticed, as it is in Liverpool.

ABIGAIL. Yeah, it's okay. (*Pause*) It's just that sometimes (Pause) I feel so lonely, with you gone most of the time. (*Fighting off tears.*) I miss you, Di'm, and it's becoming more tedious for me, with our three little children and another baby on the way. (*Her tears break through, and she begins sobbing.*) Di'm, I want to go back to Nigeria. I'll take the kids. (*Her voice trails off.*) We'll raise them in our country, where I can get a lot of help with babysitting from your mother and other relatives.

DICK TIGER, *gently wiping the tears off her face*. It is done. Your wish is my command. (*Somewhat subdued.*) I think that should be the best arrangement for now.

ABIGAL, *sobbing loudly*. I will miss you so much, Di'm, but I also know that you worry too much about me and the children. (*She suddenly becomes serious.*) I want you to focus more on your goal of becoming the world champion! I know how much you want it. It will be good for us and for our country.

DICK TIGER. Thank you, my love. By the grace of God, everything will `work out fine. I will be home frequently and will telegram you often.

ABIGAIL, *getting up and throwing her arms around him*. I love you, *ezigbo* Di'm. (My precious husband.) It shall be well. You will be victorious!

Scene Two

ABIGAIL. In America, Dick Tiger had a new manager, Wilfred "Jersey" Jones. We called him, "Jersey", and under his management, Dick was exposed to some of the best in the business, including Rory Calhoun, Joey Giardello, Gene Armstrong, Florentino Fernandez, and Henry Hank, to mention a few. He beat out all his challengers to prove his mettle, yet the chance at a world title fight eluded him. Dick was relentless in his pursuit of a chance at the world middleweight championship belt held, at the moment, by Gene Fullmer of West Jordan, Utah. He decided to go over to Jersey's office to talk things over.

(*Jersey's office is tastefully furnished, overlooking Madison Square Garden. Both sides of the wall leading to the office are adorned with framed, autographed boxing photos of some of the great boxers of the day.*)

DICK TIGER, *alone, stone-faced, he paces the room as he wonders out loud.* I have beaten out some of the best in this business, including the indomitable Henry Hank! Even after my ring victory over Gene Armstrong and Spider Webb, I have been denied the opportunity to face Fullmer in the boxing ring for the world championship! Both Armstrong and Webb, on the other hand, have had their chance to fight Fullmer for the championship. (*He pulls up a chair to sit.*) All I've gotten from Teddy Brenner ever since my astounding defeat of Henry Hank are empty promises of a chance to meet with Fullmer in the ring!...All to no avail! (*Grumbling*) I'm thirty-three years old now, and it's unfortunate that people are of the perception that boxers are "damaged goods" after they hit their thirtieth birthday! (*Gasping and folding his hands, he shakes his head.*) Boxing writers, TV and radio announcers have been very good to me, and it is evident that the public wants me to fight for the title, judging from the reception and applause I received in the Boston Arena at the third Pender-Downes encounter in April. (*Sigh*) I just need a shot at the world championship. (*Quickly*) If only I can get a shot at the middleweight championship, (*Confidently.*) I know that it will be mine! (*Jersey walks in from another room.*) Hello, Jersey.

JERSEY JONES, *startled*. Hello, Tiger.

(*Tiger gets up to shake hands with Jersey. Jersey Jones is a tactful negotiator with a long connection to boxing. A former journalist, he is a slender and youthful sixty-one-year-old New Jersey native. Both men sit.*)

JERSEY JONES. Have you been here long?

DICK TIGER, *voice subdued*. Uh, no. I just got here (*mumbles*) from a training session with Jimmy.

JERSEY JONES. Dick, I am amazed! You have exceeded expectations since dominating that fight with Rory Calhoun at Madison Square Garden. However, we need to work more on your footwork and agility in the ring. You have the strength and ability to beat out any of the top contenders, to become the world middleweight champion.

DICK TIGER, *sharply rising from his seat and putting both hands in his pants pockets*. Jersey, I was thrilled to be able to face an opponent in the famed Madison Square Garden, even though, to my dismay, the fight was ruled a draw. (*With the deepest feeling*) I know that I can become a world champion! I have beat out most of my worthy opponents, and I would like a chance to fight with the current middleweight champion, Gene Fullmer. But it looks like Fullmer and other contenders for the world championship are avoiding a matchup with me.

JERSEY JONES, *nodding*. Yes. It sure does look like they are avoiding you! (*Slight pause*) You know what? (*He gets up from his seat and moves about restlessly.*) Continue your vigorous training with Jimmy. I'll see what else we can do to get the attention of the National Boxing Association. When we get their attention through some more straight wins, then Gene Fullmer will have no option but to defend his title against you in the ring. (*Rubbing his hands together*) We are going to make them an offer.

*Dick Tiger Checking Out Boxing News with
His Manager, Wilfred "Jersey" Jones.*

DICK TIGER, *incredulously.* An offer? (*Both men sit.*) What kind of offer are we talking about?

JERSEY JONES. We are going to issue a challenge to Fullmer through the NBA commissioner, Abe Greene, including a certified check for twenty-five hundred dollars forfeit bond, challenging Fullmer to duel with you. We will also write directly to Fullmer. After we write the letter, you can then travel to Nigeria to witness the birth of your fourth "Tiger cub." I'll keep you posted on developments.

DICK TIGER, *enthused.* That sounds very good, Jersey. Let's do it!

(*The two men huddle to piece words together in order to convince Gene Fullmer to face Dick Tiger in the ring.*)

SCENE THREE

ABIGAIL. Gene Fullmer is in his manager Marv Jensen's office, and both are looking at a letter from my husband's camp.

(*Gene Fullmer and Marv Jensen are both elders in the Mormon Church. Fullmer sports a bull strong physique. He is a tough contender but pleasantly mannered. Jensen, on the other hand, is a shrewd businessman, pale-skinned and blue-eyed. Fullmer reads out loud as Jensen listens.*)

GENE FULLMER, *reading.* Dear Gene, by the time you read this, I'll be back in my native Nigeria awaiting the arrival of my latest "Tiger cub" and some news (I hope) on my challenge to you, issued through the National Boxing Association last January when I knocked out Florentino Fernandez in Miami Beach. Accompanying my challenge was a certified check of twenty-five hundred dollars posted through my agent, Jersey Jones. It is now almost three months since the challenge was posted. So far, I have heard nothing from you. I realize that your attention at the moment is centered on a possible showdown with Pender to determine which of you title claimants deserve to be recognized as undisputed world middleweight champion. As I see it, the chances of getting with Pender in the more or less immediate future are remote. There are too many problems to iron out—promoter, site, terms, etc.—and it may be months before any satisfactory deal is completed. Meanwhile, what of my challenge to you? The six-month grace period since your last defense of the NBA title will expire on June 9. That's a little over a month away. Time's wastin', Gene. I hardly need remind you that in all major ratings, I am listed as number-one contender for both yours and Pender's laurels. Naturally, I'd also like to meet Pender for his share of the title, but Pender has until October 7 before his period of grace expires. He can afford to wait a little before accepting my challenge unless, instead, he prefers meeting you first. I know you don't want any part of me in the ring, Gene, but you have a reputation to maintain. You were recognized in 1961 as the "Fighter of the Year." What are they apt to call you in 1962, if you continue to dodge your outstanding challenger? Let's hear from you, Gene. Say the word, and I'll set a speed record getting back to the United States to you. Dick Tiger, British Empire Middleweight Champion.

(Both men glance at each other, nervously. Gene drops his gaze, shoots up from his chair, and begins pacing around the room, immersed in his thoughts.)

Act Five

SCENE ONE

DICK TIGER SR. In faraway Nigeria, my wife, Abigail had given birth to our fourth child, christened, Justina. We were so proud and overjoyed. Some relatives and friends gathered to celebrate, and the ever-present foreign press and photographers were on hand too, to record the auspicious occasion. Oblivious of the events unfolding in the United States regarding my proposition to Fullmer, I relished the moment.

(*Dick Tiger's residence in Aba is a palatial, silver-gray two-story house. It is the first in a row of large-to average-sized houses on Clifford Road. Cameras are flashing. A member of the press tries to get an interview from Dick Tiger, but he will not hear of it.*)

(*Sound of baby crying*)

DICK TIGER, *to the press and photographers gathered.* Gentlemen, I ask that you please be gracious enough to leave us to tend to our newborn.

(*They reluctantly begin to leave, but not without putting in a question.*)

PRESSMAN. The great Dick Tiger, when are you ever going to return to the USA to face Gene Fullmer or Paul Pender? (*Sensing the Tiger's mood, he quietly exits.*)

DICK TIGER, *to a maid.* Please get our guests some more food and drinks. (*With arms outstretched.*) Ohh, gimme that baby. (*Another maid picks the baby up from her crib and rests her in Tiger's arms. He coos and rocks the baby back and forth.*)

Baby, baby, don't crrry. Don't crrry.

ABIGAIL, *stroking his back tenderly.* You don't want to spoil that baby with constant attention. When it's time for you to go back to the USA, she would crave that attention, which I may not be able to give, not with the other three we already have. (*She playfully grabs him from the back.*) Put her back in her crib.

DICK TIGER. Don't worry, Aby. I always picked up the other ones when they were babies, and they seem to have turned out unspoiled. (*Placing the baby on his left shoulder, he caresses her and sings a soft lullaby.*) Rock-a-bye baby on the treetop; when the wind blows, the cra—

(*There's a knock on the door. A postman enters with a telegram for Dick Tiger. He hands it to Abigail and leaves.*)

DICK TIGER. Let's hear what it says, Aby.

ABIGAIL. It's a telegram from Mr. Jones. (*Reading.*) Dear Dick, fight with Fullmer ordered by the NBA for this August. Get next flight back for training. Jersey.

DICK TIGER, *with a big grin spreading over his face.* That is great news!

ABIGAIL, *swiftly embracing her husband and baby Justina.* God has answered our prayers!

SCENE TWO

DICK TIGER SR. Jersey Jones was seated with Marv Jensen, putting the finishing touches on the contract for the impending WBA Middleweight Championship bout between Gene Fullmer and I. Jensen's reputation was that of a shrewd businessman, and he was out for his pound of flesh considering the nature and ramifications of the bout. Jersey took solace in the fact that I finally got a chance to fulfill my dreams of becoming the next world middleweight champion.

MARV JENSEN, *clearing his throat.* Okay, Jersey, you've got your wish (*Pause*) you have managed to convince the NBA of Dick Tiger's ability to vie for the world middleweight championship against Gene Fullmer. However, the agreement for the match will come with some stiff requirements. (*He raises both hands in affirmation.*) Take it, or leave it.

JERSEY JONES, *crossing his legs and leaning backward.* Well, let's hear it, Marv.

MARV JENSEN, *rising from his seat.* Now, we want at least sixty percent of the gate profits and sixty percent of the proceeds from the TV airings of the fight. On the other hand, your client, Dick Tiger, will have to settle for twenty percent of proceeds from ticket sales, or $25,000 cash and $2,700 for training expenses.

JERSEY JONES, *visibly shocked at the disparity in the amounts, he ponders the offer for another minute.* Uh, all right, Marv. We'll go along with your demands…I know how much Dick Tiger has yearned for a chance at the middleweight championship title. (*Pause.*) However, I also know that he doesn't like percentages; I'm sure he'd prefer to settle for a guarantee of the amount stated. I'll confer with Dick to ensure that it's okay with him, and then I'll get back to you.

MARV JENSEN. Very well. The tentative date for the bout is August 27 at San Francisco's Candlestick Park.

Tiger training

SCENE THREE

DICK TIGER SR. I promptly rejected the offer of twenty percent, but settled for the guaranteed sum. The fight was pushed back twice because of inclement weather and the World Series being hosted in San Francisco. Jimmy August and I, however, commenced training for the championship bout at the Catholic Youth Association (CYO) gym. The ambiance at the CYO gym was airy and conducive for training. It was devoid of the seemingly endless traffic of boxers and patrons that is the norm in most gyms in New York City.

(Dick is in a sparring session while Jimmy August looks on. They have a good working relationship, and Jimmy's expertise is not hampered by his robust stature.)

JIMMY AUGUST. C'mon, Dick, move those legs faster! You've got to be able to move away from jabs! Move those legs! Let's go! You should be able to jab and move in split seconds! (*Dick follows the directives, jabbing quickly at his beleaguered sparring partner.*) Keep pounding shots to the head and body! Go! Go! Good job!

JERSEY JONES, *walking into the gym.* Hey, guys, how's it goin'?

JIMMY AUGUST, *motioning to the sparring partner.* Take five. (*To Tiger*) Come 'ere a minute, Tiger.

DICK TIGER, *Tiger moves toward Jersey and Jimmy.* Hello Jersey.

JERSEY JONES. I've got good news (*Pause*) and bad news (*He adjusts his trousers.*) The good news is earnings from ticket sales for this fight are expected to be higher. (*Straightening himself, he puts his hands on his waist.*) The bad news is the bout has been postponed to October 16.

DICK TIGER and JIMMY AUGUST, *in unison.* Again?

DICK TIGER. This is the third postponement. (*Skeptical*) Are you sure that I am ever going to get a shot at the world championship? Maybe it was all just a dream (*Pauses*) at first, it was the twenty-seventh of August, then the sixteenth of September, now this new date? (*Bewildered*) I don't know. (*Pause*) What's going on?

JERSEY JONES. It'll happen, Dick. You'll get your day in the ring with Fullmer. This latest postponement is because of weather conditions imminent in the city of San Francisco at this time of year. The first postponement was because of the Cuban Missile crisis. Then, there was a conflict in scheduling at the site. It should be resolved soon, Dick. Just stay focused on your workout and training regimen.

JIMMY AUGUST, *patting him on the shoulders*. Yeah! Cheer up, Tiger. Hey, your friends are here for you, even the chief cabinet member for sports in your country has promised to fly in just to show his support. They have every confidence in you to win this crown. You can't let them or your country, down.

Scene Four

DICK TIGER SR. Nigeria's minister of labor, Chief Joseph Modupe Johnson (JMJ), arrived in San Francisco, along with my good friend, Hogan Bassey. The day before the middleweight championship fight, I received a telegraphed goodwill missive from the governor-general of Nigeria, Dr. Nnamdi Azikiwe. He was surrounded by the colorful Nigerian minister of sports, Chief JMJ, and Hogan Bassey, Nigeria's premiere world-champion boxer. Hogan Bassey and I shared the same interests. His charm and youthful exuberance complemented my reserved but congenial nature.

DICK TIGER, *reading a letter from Dr. Azikiwe.*

It is with great pleasure that I send this message of cheer, comfort and goodwill on behalf of myself, my government, and the people of Nigeria, your beloved country. I know you will do your best and you will observe the rules of the game as you enter the squared ring to vie for fistic glory. No matter what happens, let your worthy opponent know that he has fought the fight of his life. May fortune smile on you, but hit hard and defend yourself in the tradition of the manly art. Good luck, Dick Tiger.

DICK TIGER, *standing, with conviction*. I am deeply touched by the support and encouragement of my people. (*His voice trails off.*) Victory shall surely be ours. I will bring home the glory to Nigeria! (*Bassey and JMJ quickly stand to give Tiger a hug.*)

HOGAN BASSEY. We know that you can do it! You will be world champion, by the grace of God.

CHIEF JMJ, *raising Tiger's left hand.* You will make us proud, Dick Tiger. You know it! We know it!

SCENE FIVE

GOLDSMITH. The skies opened up, and the rains continued to pour profusely, causing landslides and fatalities. As a result, the fight was pushed further up to the final date of October 23, 1962. Present at ringside were Dick Tiger's old friends and associates from Liverpool, England, and a delegation from the Federal Republic of Nigeria, led by Nigeria's sports minister, Chief Joseph Modupe Johnson (JMJ) and Hogan "Kid" Bassey. A group of Nigerian students were rounded up by Jersey Jones to be part of the rooting section for Dick Tiger. The fight lasted the full fifteen rounds.

(*At Candlestick Park in San Francisco*)

ANNOUNCER, *after the national anthems, with a microphone, standing in the center of the stage.* Laaadies and gentllllllemen, the world middleweight championship belt is up for grabs! Today's bout is between the challengers for the world middleweight championship, Dick Tiger of Nigeriaa! (*Cheers and applause*).

(*Tiger steps out with his left fist raised, does a 360-degree twirl, acknowledging the cheers of the crowd.*)

ANNOUNCER. And, the reigning world middleweight champion, Gene Fullllllllllmer! (*Cheers.*)

(*Fullmer enters the stage, wearing white boxing trunks with hands raised in greeting to the crowd. The bell rings, and the men begin to duel.*)

GOLDSMITH. Fullmer lived up to his reputation as "The Brawler." He came charging into Dick Tiger, throwing shots, almost overwhelming him, but Tiger blocked his wild punches and responded by standing his ground and connecting his gloved fists to Fullmer's head and body. In rounds two and three, both scored evenly. In the third and fourth rounds, they did too, but with Tiger winning on points. Round five, Tiger's stinging left hook put a gash on Fullmer's forehead. Blood oozed down his brow, covering his eyes. In round eight, Tiger's head butted into Fullmer's, worsening the cut, causing blood to flow profusely. A ringside physician attended to the cut. Despite the injuries, Fullmer plodded on. Rounds five through eleven were judged in Tiger's favor. Rounds twelve, thirteen, and fourteen were also awarded to Dick Tiger. By all accounts, Tiger was winning. In the fifteenth and final round, Dick Tiger dominated the fight and won, snatching the middleweight championship from the only man to beat Sugar Ray Robinson unanimously.

ANNOUNCER, *bell sounds, and the boxers stand together in the ring.*

Laaaadies and gentlemen! We have a new world middleweight champion! (*The crowd roars.*) Dick Tiiiiiger! (*There's a drumbeat and jubilation. Tiger waves to the crowd, as his elated fans storm into the ring and hoist him onto their shoulders.*)

Dick Tiger is hoisted on the shoulders of his fans and admirers after he clinched the world middleweight title from Gene Fullmer in1962. On the left is Chief RBK Okafor, a distinguished member of the Nigerian Parliament and Chief JMJ (right) beaming in smiles.

GENE FULLMER, *right after Tiger's victory is announced in the ring; with face all bloodied, he walks toward Jersey Jones.* You've got a great champion in Dick Tiger.

JERSEY JONES, *patting him on the back.* Thank you, Gene. Great fight.

GENE FULLMER, *hurriedly walks toward Dick Tiger)* Congratulations, Dick Tiger. You are a worthy champion.

DICK TIGER, *smiling broadly, he pats Gene on the back.* Thanks, Gene. Thanks for granting me the privilege. (*He promptly exits, as a score of reporters hound him for interviews.*)

SCENE SIX

GOLDSMITH. After the reporters disperse, the two champions met.

DICK TIGER. Gene, since you were sportsman enough to give me a crack at the world-championship title, I want to be just as gracious and grant you the opportunity of a rematch if and when you want it. (*Assuredly*) I will not decide anything definite about future bouts until I hear from you regarding this proposition.

GENE FULLMER, *visibly moved*. I appreciate that, Dick. I'll decide as soon as possible what my next course of action will be (*Slight pause*), and you will be the first to know what I decide to do about a rematch.

DICK TIGER. Very good. Take care. (*He exits. Gene stands alone, pensive.*)

GENE FULLMER. What a guy. (*Pause.*) I am grateful and feel a great sense of pride for my enviable accomplishments in this field (*pauses*) I've boxed with some of the best in this business, including the indomitable Sugar Ray Robinson, and I've beat each one of them! Me, a simple boy from West Jordan (*Transfixed*). I boxed and beat the legendary "Sugar Man!" (*Shaking his head violently, as if snapping out of a trance, he looks around to make sure no one was watching.*) I'll give my facial wounds some time to heal before I take on this African battler called Dick Tiger. (*Pause.*) He seems a neat guy, a fine gentleman, not to mention that he packs a mean punch! (*Wrinkling his face.*) But you know, if I had to lose this championship, I cannot think of a better man to lose it to than this boxing enigma, Dick Tiger. (*He adjusts his blazer and walks off.*)

SCENE SEVEN

GOLDSMITH. The Nigerian delegation, confident of Dick Tiger's eminent win of the world championship, prearranged a victory party in his honor. The party was organized by Chief JMJ and hosted at the Mark Hopkins Club in San Francisco. At the rollicking scene, Chief JMJ toasted Dick Tiger's victory. The carousing and merriment continued all night long.

(*At the Mark Hopkins Club,*)

CHIEF JMJ, *holding Tiger's left hand up; he raises a glass of wine with the other hand and thunders.* To the champion! (*Still holding the champ's left hand up, he turns to the guests.*) Our champion! Your champion! Everybody's champion!

GUESTS, *singing.* For he's a jolly good fellow! For he's a jolly good fellow! For he's a jolly good fellooww! Which nobody can denyyyy!

(*Applause and cheers.*)

DICK TIGER, *blushing, he flashes a set of pearly white teeth.* Thank you. Thank you very much!

CHIEF JMJ. Eat! Drink! And be merry!

(*A live band blasts a mix of African and Calypso rhythms. Champagne flows from the bar, and the buffet section offers a spread of multinational delicacies.*)

SCENE EIGHT

GOLDSMITH. It was 2.30 a.m. Outside of the Mark Hopkins Club, guests were starting to exit. Some guests, however, like Mr. Wulite, a member of the Nigerian delegation, was finding it difficult to coordinate hand and body movements. His colleague, Mr. Talade, came to the rescue. Both men are middle-aged and of a slim build, but Mr. Wulite has a visibly large Adam's apple that protrudes from the walls of his neck, and throbs wildly upwards and downwards when he gulps!

(*Outside of the club, the inebriated Mr. Wulite is still clutching a bottle of wine as he tries in vain to walk.*)

MR. WULITE. Eh, chei! (*Oh, wow!*) (*He smiles, with mouth agape and tongue hanging outside of his mouth.*) Notin' betta than a good plate of nkwobi (*spicy beef stew*) and gogoro bekee—chappayne! (*He loosely examines the bottle and shoots out his lips to a pucker.*) Mmm! Oh! (*Raising the bottle to his lips, he takes a sip and then tilts his head back and gulps, downing the bubbling drink.*) Ahhhh! Oh! (*He peers at the half-empty bottle, quickly clamps it to his mouth, and wrapping anxious lips around it, takes long, excited gulps. His left fingers mysteriously develop a mind and conscience of their own, and as he gulps, each trembling finger runs with wild devotion across his chest and belly, finally settling on his, crotch. He grabs and tugs.*) Ahhhh! Chei! (*In an explosion of unbridled joy, he begins to rock from side to side, still cupping his crotch with restless fingers and wiggling his body.*) Ohhh! Zara muo o! Zarrrah! Ohh! (*The wiggling action is growing more intense now.*)

MR. TALADE, *noticing Mr. Wulite.* Stop! What are you doing? (*Mr. Wulite is startled and falls on his behind. Mr. Talade helps him up and pulls the bottle away from him.*) Give me that! (*He pours the remaining contents on the paved street.*)

MR. WULITE, *disheveled, speech slurred.* Ta-take your hands off. (*Pauses*)

Gimme back that bottttle (*Pause*) befo I punch you like De Tiga

punch Fullma! Give it 'ere! (*He strikes a quasi-boxing pose, inviting Mr. Talade to fight. Reluctantly, Mr. Talade hands over the empty bottle. Grabbing the empty bottle, Mr. Wulite plunges it under his arm, pressing it tight under his sweating armpit. He begins hiccupping.*) Befo I (*hiccups*) box you (*mumbles*) like Tiga box Ful-lu-ma! (*Disoriented and desperately trying to adjust his traditional attire -agbada, he staggers.*) I say notin' betta than a good plate of nkwobi (*mumbles*) and gogoro bekee–chappayne! (*Gently whirling his tongue around his lips*) Sweet Zara! *(Hiccups)* Zaraahrrah! Ohhh! *(He begins to rock himself again.)*

MR. TALADE, *getting frustrated, shrieks.* Your Zara is not here! They didn't even serve nkwobi; it was filet mignon that you ate! (*Noticing some passersby staring, he hangs his head in shame.*) This is embarrassing! (*Mumbles*) Come (*He struggles to help Mr. Wulite walk straight.*) You're as drunk as a skunk! You're going back to the hotel.

MR. WULITE, *still drunk, eyes half shut.* You mean (*mumbles*) that wassint nkwobi?

MR. TALADE, *slightly amused.* No, it wasn't!

MR. WULITE, *pausing, he grins faintly.* Chei! Oyibo eh! (*Holding the bottle out, as if far-sighted, he examines it, smacks his lips, and feels his lips with his tongue, again.*) That *ogogoro bekee,* (*halts*) sweet chappayne, (*pauses*) like sweet Zara beke! Chei! (*Mechanically, he lays the bottle on the floor and grabs his crotch again, with both hands.*) Za rah rah ehhh! (*Grunting.*) Zararah! Ahhhr! (*Groaning.*) Za mu'o! Zaramu oohh! Aayyiii!

MR. TALADE, *growing irritated, quickly hails a cab)* Taxi! Governor Hotel! (*Pulling Mr. Wulite by his disheveled agbada, he moves toward the taxi.*) Let's go!

Act Six

SCENE ONE

DICK TIGER SR. Exhausted from the revelry that followed my victory and induction into the world boxing championship ranks, I took a long nap. When I awoke late in the morning, I put a much-anticipated call to my dear wife, Abigail, and later touched base with my brothers.

ABIGAIL, *the phone rings; she picks it up.* Hello

DICK TIGER, *affectionately.* Aby, my wife—

ABIGAIL, *happily.* Oh, my gosh! Di'm! (*She breaks into a song.*) Blessed be the name of the Lord! Blessed be the name of the Looord! Blessed be the name of the Lord most highhhh!

(*Dick Tiger joins in.*)

DICK TIGER and ABIGAIL. The name of the Lord is (*pause*) a strong towerrrrr! The righteous run into it, and they are saved! The name of the Lord is, a strong tow-errrr! The righteous run into it, and they are saved! Blessed be the name of the Lord! Blessed be the name of the Looord! Blessed be the name of the Lord, most highhhh! The name of the Lord is a strong tow-errrrrr! The righteous run into it, and they are saaaaaved! (*They laugh warmly.*)

ABIGAIL. My husband, congratulations! You have done well. I know how much you had dreamed of becoming a world champion. Your dream has materialized. Thank God! Everybody in the city—in fact, in the whole country— is ecstatic about your winning the world championship! (*Speaking very fast and excitedly.*) Look, even the Ekeoha market traders abandoned their wares in the market to roam the streets chanting, "Nzogbu! Nzogbu! Enyimba! Enyi! Nzogbu! Enyimba! Enyi!" (*She pauses slightly.*) People have been carousing since your win! (*Laughing warmly.*) Your picture with your big nose and broad smile is plastered all over the place! (*They giggle, and she continues.*) The phone has been ringing off the hook. Everybody who's anybody has called, from the governor- general to ministers and, of course, your relatives far and near. They are so proud of you! (*She pauses, before continuing, giving great weight to each word.*) You have reunited this country (*mumbles*) if only for a few days! (*She pauses, sensing he might be tired.*) Are you okay, Di'm?

DICK TIGER, *,smiling faintly.* I'm okay, just exhausted from all the autograph-signing, the handshaking, and the merriment. Phew! (*Jokingly.*) My hand is not sore from boxing with Fullmer, but from all the handshaking and autograph-signing (*Both laugh*).

ABIGAIL. I can't wait for you to come home so that I can make your favorite foods for you. You must be craving some good *achi* and *onugbu* soup!

DICK TIGER. I can't wait to see you and my babies. How are they holding up? I know they must be startled by all the attention. Please keep them closer to you, especially Vicky, my crybaby. Make sure she's insulated from all the commotion.

ABIGAIL. When will you be home?

DICK TIGER. Right after I wrap up some engagements here. I should be home before December, just in time for Christmas with you guys.

ABIGAIL. Try to come back as soon as you can. I need your help in attending to the endless stream of visitors.

DICK TIGER. I will send a telegram to my brothers. They should have knowledge of my itinerary when I come home. Please stay strong for me and the children. We need you. I need you! Bye. (*He hangs up and begins to draft a telegram to his brothers.*)

Scene Two

GOLDSMITH. Dick Tiger, my great friend, returned to his homeland to a congested schedule of events enough to overwhelm even a presidential candidate in an election year. He was now an A-list celebrity, a national icon, and for the rest of his life will continue to receive reverential treatment. In celebration of his arrival, the Aba Urban council arranged a grand welcome. Thousands of people lined a seven-mile stretch of the Onitsha-Aba Highway, all the way to his house, singing and dancing. The next day, he stood in a sun-roofed vehicle at the head of a motorcade. A line of admirers, some of whom had been waiting for hours, stretched from his house on Clifford Road to the Aba Sports Stadium, where he was treated to an overdose of entertainment.

(*At Dick Tiger's residence in Aba.*)

DICK TIGER, *addressing the crowd from the balcony of his home.* Kedu nu? (*How are you?*) I appreciate your love and devotion very much. (*Screams of Tiga! Tiga!*) I promise to continue to make you proud. Please continue to work hard in everything that you do. And remember to always pray for our country, even as you pray for yourselves and your families. (*He brings out bundles of money and hands them over to the leader of the group, bidding them farewell. Schoolchildren among the group break into a song and joyfully parade around his house for a few more minutes.*)

PARADE OF SCHOOL CHILDREN, *singing*. I saw Dick Tiger in the newspaper! The world champion! Of Nigeria! I saw Dick Tiger in the newspaper; he was fighting Gene Fullmarrr! God bless the name of Dick Tiger! For fighting Gene Fullmarrr! Who was fighting Tiger for the middleweight, in the name of the USAAA!

Scene Three

GOLDSMITH. DICK TIGER'S stay in Nigeria continued to be marked by endless invitations to social gatherings. He had realized that his newfound fame brought with it a substantial measure of influence and responsibility. Seizing on this reckoning, he threw his world-champion weight on some worthy social issues plaguing the country. Here he addressed a community-based organization in Enugu, the capital of the eastern region before heading back to America.

Dr. Nnamdi Azikiwe and the premier of the Eastern Region,
Eze Ogo Afikpo, Akanu Ibiam (right) pose with Dick Tiger
during a courtesy call at the governor-general's residence.

(At Enugu, the capital city of Nigeria's eastern region, Tiger addresses
some government officials, while emphasizing the importance of youth
empowerment.)

DICK TIGER, *to the audience.* It is my pleasure to be here with you
today. You are one of the strongest pillars of our community
and must try to uphold the honor reposed in you. Our youth
are the future of our country, and we must ensure that they
receive all the nurturing and education they need to become
useful citizens of Nigeria, to be able to impact their families
and their communities (*Applause*). I can wholly identify with
the plight of our youth today, because I was once like them,
(*pauses*) right here in Enugu. (*Nodding in affirmation of this
disclosure.*) I have walked in the same shoes that they are
walking in right now, and I know firsthand that it is not easy,
and they need our support in order to grab their destiny in their
hands! (*Applause*) I appeal to our leaders in the communities,
the state and federal houses, to devise ways to combat the high

rate of youth unemployment, especially in the eastern region. We urge the government to research ways to capitalize on the abundant resources derived from palm nut and palm wine. (*Pause*) Improved harvesting and production methods in the palm oil and palm wine-making industry will help to create jobs, especially for the urban poor. We hope for a brighter future for one and for all. (*They clap.*) When I am fighting in the ring, I must always think of Nigeria! (*Clapping continues.*) Thank you all for this warm reception and for allowing me to address some important issues that plague our communities today. (*Pause*) I am also going to put my money where my mouth is by supporting the youth employment initiative with a donation of ten thousand pounds. (*He receives a thunderous applause, standing ovation, and screams of "Tiga! Tiga!"*)

Scene Four

DICK TIGER SR. Back in America, Paul Pender, another WBA middleweight championship contender, had been clamoring for a match with me since my win against Fullmer, but when this didn't happen, Pender abruptly gave up his middleweight championship bid. British promoters, Jack Solomons and Harry Levine, also offered a lucrative rematch with the popular Terry Downes, but feeling indebted to Fullmer, I kept my promise of a rematch with him. In West Jordan, Utah, Fullmer conceded to a rematch and had devised a strategy he, along with his manager, believed would give Fullmer an edge in the ring over and against me. A date for the match was scheduled to occur on February 23 of the next year, 1963, at the Convention Hall in Las Vegas, Nevada,.

(*In Marv Jensen's office*)

GENE FULLMER, *with a smirk.* Marv, I think I have found the secret to beating Dick Tiger this time around.

MARV JENSEN, *intrigued.* Mmmm, do tell, Gene. How d'ya figure we can beat this slugger to regain the middleweight crown?

GENE FULLMER, *mysteriously.* There's something in Tiger's style that will suit me the next time we duel. (*Slight laugh*) I figured it out in the last rounds of our first fight! (*Leaning forward*) I'll just hold him off until much later into the rounds. I'll keep evading him and holding him off (*mumbles*) until he gets irritated and tired of stalking me. (*His eyes glisten.*) Then, (*excitedly*) when he's worn out from chasing me around the ring, (*smirks*) like a wounded tiger, (*both men snicker*) then (*Gesturing*) I'll begin to crowd him, jab him, and retreat. (*Demonstrating.*) Crowd him, jab, and retreat. Crowd, jab, and retreat.

MARV JENSEN, *smiling wryly.* In your first fight with him, he made you fight his kind of fight—stand and deliver! (*They chuckle.*)

GENE FULLMER, *emphasizing.* But this time, we'll make him fight our kind of fight: crowd him, jab, and retreat.

BOTH. Crowd, jab and retreat! Crowd, jab, and retreat!

MARV JENSEN, *nodding affirmatively and wringing his hands.* This is ingenious, Gene! I think it'll work! (*Smirking*) We know how he dreads (*smirking*) having to move…. briskly on stage. (*Gazing intently into Fullmer's eyes, he snaps.*) You might win the championship back from that Tiger after all, Utah Bully Boy! (*They cackle.*)

SCENE FIVE

DICK TIGER SR. FULLMER stayed true to his plan to wrestle the title back from me. However, the rematch ended in a bruising fifteen-round draw, and Fullmer, who had earlier indicated a willingness to retire if he lost again to me, was emboldened by the draw and requested another match with me.

Bracing for another showdown with Gene Fullmer

(After the rematch in Las Vegas, the boxers confer.)

GENE FULLMER. Dick Tiger, you were gracious enough to permit me a rematch after I lost the middleweight championship to you. I was contemplating a retirement from boxing if I lost to you again on our second meet, but now that there is a draw, I think you should be man enough to give me another crack at the title *(pauses)* If you think that you deserve this middleweight title unequivocally, then you should give the nod for our third duel.

DICK TIGER. I'm a man of my word, Gene. I gladly grant you another opportunity to wrestle the title from me, if you can. (*Pause*) I am a true champion and will give my opponent every opportunity to prove his mettle against mine in the ring, until an undisputed champion emerges. (*Proudly*) If I am to be champion, it has to be by unanimous decision (*pauses*) undisputed (*Punctuated*) proven champion of the world.

GENE FULLMER. You got it, Tiger. (*The two men shake hands.*) It's a deal. (*They exit*)

Act Seven

SCENE ONE

ABIGAIL. AS soon as the result of the second match was announced, boxing promoters from other parts of the world, sensing an even more bountiful harvest to be reaped from a third bout between the two well-matched boxers, converged with offers of large sums to promote a third meet. Jersey Jones consulted with my husband, Dick Tiger, and his trainer, Jimmy August.

(*At the CYO Gym*)

JERSEY JONES, *surprised.* It's amazing the kind of interest this contest has generated. I am getting offers from all these promoters. Some have offered as much as $150,000 to showcase the third bout between Tiger and Gene! (*Speaking very quickly.*) As if that's not shocking enough, I received a telegraphed message from Dick Tiger's country of Nigeria! They also would like a shot at hosting the world title bout.

DICK TIGER, *elated.* That's great! Africa should be given the opportunity to host a world-championship bout, and Nigeria, as my beloved country—the giant of Africa— should be granted that privilege!

JIMMY AUGUST, *carefully, delicately.* Now (*hesitatingly*) Dick, I don't think that's such a good idea. Remember, Africa is thousands of miles away. It's too hot over there, and I don't think the natives will be able to understand our kind of English—

DICK TIGER, *slightly irritated.* Oh please, Jimmy. If you can communicate with me, then you can communicate with any (*exaggeratedly*) of the people in Nigeria. We are definitely not going to walk there; we are going to fly in a commercial airplane. (*Amused*) You think we are all cannibals over there, hah, Jimmy? (*Animatedly*) We eat humoan [human] beings, hah? (*Quickly*) You think that we are Tarzans and swing from tree to tree, hah?

JIMMY AUGUST, *flustered.* Don't be silly, Tiger. These are honest concerns. I am not being frivolous. It's just that it's never been done before. *(pause)* A world championship, in Africa?

JERSEY JONES. Hang on, gentlemen. (*Swallowing hard.*) The telegram came from a committee calling themselves the "Dick Tiger–Gene Fullmer Fight Campaign Committee." Their goal is to petition the Nigerian Federal Government to sponsor the bout. (*Pause.*) I do have my reservations, but they are persistent. We'll see what happens.

DICK TIGER, *abruptly.* What will happen is that we will host the fight in my beautiful country of Nigeria!

JERSEY JONES. We're talking $100,000 to $150,000 figures offered to host in the US now. (*Pause*) It's somewhat doubtful that there is that kind of money for a fight in Nigeria. (*Throwing both hands in the air.*) If they think they can do it, of course we're interested. But there are certainly a lot of logistics and ramifications to consider.

DICK TIGER, *slightly irritated.* Jersey, it's going to be done. (*Pause*)
If Nigeria wants to host this next fight between Gene and me,
then I am sure they can meet any required obligations. Thank
you. (*There's silence, as each man briefly glances at the others.*)

Scene Two

ABIGAIL. My husband, Dick Tiger, put a call through to me.
We talked about our kids, and discussed Nigeria's increasing
interest in staging the next world-championship fight in
Nigeria. The public consensus in Nigeria was that Dick Tiger
had been cheated out of a clean win against Fullmer. The
majority of the politicians, reporters, and the populace in
Nigeria want the fight staged on their turf, where they feel
that there would be less chances of a rig in the final decision.

(*At Dick Tiger's residence, the phone rings. Abigail picks up.*)

ABIGAIL. Hello.

DICK TIGER. Hello, Aby. How are you, my wife?

ABIGAIL. I'm fine, and how are you getting on over there?

DICK TIGER. Good. How is the baby? Is she recovering from
the high fever?

ABIGAIL. She's fine now. The only problem is that she is very
precocious. Since she took her first steps, she has insisted on
moving about on her own. She kicks and screams if you try to
restrain her. Grace and Vicky are her favorite playmates. The
only time that I or her sitter, Ozioma, are able to unwind is
when she is sleeping or playing with her sisters.

DICK TIGER. That's good. What about my son, Richard? Put
him on the phone for me. Hope he gets along with his siblings.

ABIGAIL. Oh, he is a big boy. (*She brings Richard Jr. to the phone.*)

DICK TIGER, *to son.* Junior, how are you doing?

RICHARD JR. Papa! Are you coming home tomorrow?

DICK TIGER. Not quite yet, but I'll be home real soon. I'll buy you some more toys but only if you promise to help your mother in taking care of your sisters.

RICHARD JR. I promise.

DICK TIGER. See you, son.

RICHARD JR. Okay, Papa. Bye-bye.

ABIGAIL. He keeps mostly to himself, playing with his toys and cars. But he tries to help when needed. Especially with his twin, he is always willing to assist her in learning her sign language and helps in keeping her focused.

DICK TIGER. That's good. Grace is almost four years old; when she turns five, I will hire a fulltime special education teacher to homeschool her. For high school, she will be enrolled in that reputable school for the deaf in Lagos. (*Pause*) She can become anything that she wants to become in life—even with that handicap. (*Brightening up.*) Hope they liked the stuff I shipped home to them earlier.

ABIGAIL. Oh, yes. Too many toys though. Please don't spoil them. Nobody wants a spoiled brat.

DICK TIGER. No, I won't spoil them. Just missing all of you so much. What about my brothers and their families? How are they? I hope they make time to visit you and the kids.

ABIGAIL. Everybody is fine. I saw them just two days ago. (*Perking up*) Now, how about this fight? A lot of people in the country feel, as I do, that you were robbed of a clean win!

DICK TIGER. Oh, Abby, I know they must be hurt that their champion did not win this time (*He smiles.*), but I win most of the time. It was another tough fight, and the judges felt the best thing to do would be to rule it a draw. (*Pause*) Thank God there will be a next time.

ABIGAIL, *gushing.* You are ever a good sport, My champion husband! (*Tiger blushes.*) Have you started your training regimen? News is the federal government would like to see the fight hosted here in Nigeria? (*Animated*) Oh, I sure hope that materializes. It'd be great to have you closer to home, if only for a few months at a time!

DICK TIGER. That would be great. Hosting a world title fight would be good for our fledgling country. The world has to know, through this hosting, that Nigeria and indeed Africa are not inundated with cannibals and rain forests. They have to realize that Nigeria is a modern country with basic amenities and, yes, the intellect to pull off the hosting of a world title event. I will ring up my friend at the United Nations, Chief Adebo. He should be able to help impress upon the international scene the need to have Nigeria host this match.

ABIGAIL. Certainly! There's even an ad hoc committee already working with the minister of labor, Chief Johnson, to ensure that Nigeria does not miss out on this golden opportunity. There are some dissidents, however, who feel that it'd be a waste of much needed resources, an exercise in futility.

DICK TIGER. All we can do is keep working hard to convince them otherwise. I will train harder. I want to win this time by a technical knockout! The rest of the Western world has to begin to respect Africa. We want most of the same things they want for their countries and their children.

ABIGAIL. I know you can win it, and through your victory in this historic match, a lot of misgivings about our people will be busted! (*Gently*) Now, don't you go stressing yourself out. Continue to trust in the Lord, and may He continue to take the lead in your life.

DICK TIGER. Amen. It is well. I love you, Aby. Take good care of yourself and the kiddies. I will see you guys soon, God-willing.

ABIGAIL. Okay, my husband. May the Good Lord continue to bless you.

DICK TIGER, *before hanging up.* And you, my wife. I love you. Bye.

SCENE THREE

ABIGAIL. The Nigerian ambassador to the United Nations, Chief Adebo, flew into Nigeria for a meeting with Prime Minister Tafawa Balewa at the invitation of Chief Johnson. At Prime Minister Balewa's office, the topic of discussion was the possibility of Nigeria hosting the impending Tiger versus Fullmer fight.

(*At Alhaji Abubakar Tafawa Balewa's office in Lagos, Chief JMJ and Chief Adebo enter. The prime minister is slightly built, middle-aged, and soft-spoken, with a tribal mark on his left cheek.*)

CHIEFS ADEBO and JMJ. Good morning, Your Excellency.

PM BALEWA. Good morning, Joseph. Hello, Simeon. (*Offering them seats.*) My secretary informed me that you had an urgent matter to discuss. (*Straightening his agbada.*) What is it?

CHIEF JMJ, *swallowing hard.* Your Excellency, the country is buzzing with news of Dick Tiger's fight with Fullmer.

PM BALEWA, *credulously.* We all know that they fought to a draw in Las Vegas. Have they decided on a date for a rematch?

CHIEF JMJ, *saying each word slowly.* Your Excellency, the majority of Nigerians do not think that that fight was judged fairly.

CHIEF ADEBO, *quickly.* And they are agitating, through the press and their legislators, for a rematch between Dick Tiger and Fullmer to be held right here in Nigeria.

PM BALEWA, *pause.* Joseph, Simeon, where are we going to hold this fight? (*Shaking his head.*) I do not know how practical this venture would be considering that (*hesitates*) I don't think that we have adequate financial and infrastructural resources to cope with the tremendous demands an event of such scale would entail. We won our independence from British rule barely three years ago, and the country now has a lot of social and economic needs, which we are hoping to ameliorate through the implementation of the Six-Year Development Plan inaugurated just last year.

CHIEF JMJ, *undeterred.* Your Excellency, it will be quite practical to host the fight here in Nigeria. It would be good for Nigeria, in particular, and Africa, in general. Since we are a new nation, this could be our chance to prove to the world, especially to our former colonizers that we have truly achieved sovereignty status and can hold our own with any other country on the globe. (*Giving great weight to each word.*) Hosting the Tiger versus Fullmer fight in Nigeria would bring our country much-needed recognition and prestige. (*Assuredly.*) Your Excellency, this fight promises to put our country on the world map!

CHIEF ADEBO, *interjecting.* And consider this, Your Excellency, hosting this championship would be in line with the ideology of the Six-Year Plan. We are, in essence, improving and enhancing our country's image and conversely, the world's perception of our country as a competent ally and partner in trade relations, etc. (*Thoughtfully*) We know how passionate you are about banning atomic bomb testing in the Sahara Desert, and our country is currently involved in talks with America over the adoption of the Test Ban Treaty, which resumed this June. Our ability to pull off this historic event would prove us worthy allies in global trade negotiations and international policy developments.

PM BALEWA, *struggling*. Gentlemen, you have put forth a very good argument, but I don't know how easy it will be to convince the rest of the members of parliament that it is such a rewarding venture.

CHIEF JMJ, *slightly amused*. Please, allow me to disclose that an overwhelming number of our legislators want the Tiger-Fullmer fight to happen here, in our country. (*Pause.*) It will be good not only for our country but for the rest of Black Africa. (*Adjusting his glasses*) Apartheid South Africa, which has perpetually sanctioned discrimination against black Africans (*Emphasizing*) in their own country, has hosted world-championship bouts. We will be making history by being the first *real* African country to host a world championship event—and with one of our own, Dick Tiger as a principal player. (*Nodding in affirmation.*) I know the citizens of Nigeria want this, as does the rest of Black Africa.

CHIEF ADEBO. Same goes for our citizens living and studying abroad, especially in the USA. The general consensus among them is that it would be a splendid idea to have our own Dick Tiger fight in his native country while he's still the world champion.

PM BALEWA. *agreeably*. Very well. Let's pray that our brother, Dick Tiger, will win again—this time by a knockout!

CHIEF JMJ, *elated*. Yes, Your Excellency! He is very capable. He will get that win by a knockout!

Nigerian visionaries—exponents of the Tiger versus Fullmer III showcase. From left is Chief Obafemi Awolowo, Dr. Nnamdi Azikiwe (center) and Alhaji Abubakar Tafawa Balewa.

PM BALEWA, *pensively*. This fight will be the first of its kind in the whole of Africa, and that is sure to bring our fledgling country some respect globally. The event will also empower our citizens to aspire to become as great as Dick Tiger in their individual endeavors. (*Motioning to Chief JMJ.*) Get the papers ready *(pauses)* In my capacity as the prime minister of this great nation, I promise my unwavering support to bringing the Tiger versus Fullmer fight to the shores of Africa, in Nigeria's honor, in Africa's honor.

CHIEF JMJ. I will do that, Your Excellency.

CHIEF ADEBO. Thank you for your time, and I will see you in New York, Your Excellency, when you visit the USA again.

PM BALEWA. Yes. I will be meeting with President Kennedy at the White house in a few weeks. (*He smiles.*) You are doing marvelously well in your new designation as Nigeria's foreign ambassador to the United Nations. Keep up the good work.

CHIEF ADEBO. Thank you, Your Excellency. I appreciate that.

PM BALEWA, *to Chief JMJ*. You are great too, Joseph, in your capacity as the minister charged with sports and youth development in the country. (*Pause*) It's been a pleasure, gentlemen. (*Getting up to shake their hands.*) Go out there and let's make it work!

CHIEFS ADEBO and JMJ. Thank you, Your Excellency. (*They leave.*)

Scene Four

ABIGAIL. The campaign for Nigeria to host the world championship began to gather a lot of steam and had morphed into a demonstration of national pride and a patriotic duty. In the streets of Lagos, Nigeria, members of the "Fight-at-Home" team, made up of editors from various national newspapers, carry placards publicizing their demands. The spokesperson stood on a makeshift podium to address the crowd of onlookers that are gathering. Some signs read: "FIGHT AT HOME, NOW !" Others read, "PRESTIGE FOR NIGERIA, NOW!" while some read, "COME TO NATION'S RESCUE, BALEWA !" And some, "FULLMER VS. TIGER IN NIGERIA!" Their efforts did not go unnoticed, as members of the public join in to voice their desires to the powers that be. Groups were pitted against each other. Is the country ready, amidst its socio-economic issues, to stage a momentous world title event?

(*On a popular street in Lagos, a tall, chubby, middle–aged man mounts the podium carrying an enlarged poster of Dick Tiger's visage super imposed on a map of the African continent. He eloquently uses his raspy voice, punctuated with intense concentration, to drive his message home to his captivated audience.*)

SPOKESPERSON FOR THE FIGHT-AT-HOME CAMPAIGN COMMITTEE, *audaciously.* Fellow Nigerians, we salute you! We ask that you please join us in the crusade to pull our country from the grips of universal humiliation, skepticism, and innuendos about our potential and integrity as a people. Let us arrest the looming darkness by bringing light! (*Clapping*) Nigeria has already produced two world-champion boxers in Hogan Bassey and Dick Tiger, yet none of them has had the opportunity to display their skills before their countrymen in their country of Nigeria. (*Stretching his hands toward the audience.*) Is that fair? (*Echoes of "No! No!"*) Now, our son, (*Pointing at the poster.*) the great Dick Tiger, is one of the principals in another world middleweight boxing championship bout. We want our son to bring his partners and the rest of the world to the shores of Africa, to our beloved country of Nigeria! (*Applause.*) We are not brutes or cannibals. We are not barbaric. We do not live in trees, and yes, we may have some mud huts, but we also have some palace-styled mansions. (*Echoes of "Yes! Yes!"*) Let us invite the world to a world-championship event on our shores in Africa. Let us show the world, courtesy of our son, Dick Tiger, that Africans are as versatile and as endowed as the rest of the human race! (*Thunderous applause. He pauses.*) We are grateful for the democracy that we have in our country, which accords opposing viewpoints the same leverage. (*Incredulously.*) That bunch would rather it happen in another country, far away from the African shores! They call it (*Exaggerating.*), "a waste of municipal funds!" (*Pause*) "Prodigal!" "A homicidal game!" (*Louder*) They miss the mark! (*Applause. He pauses.*) The privilege to host this match of epic proportions is invaluable! (*Wagging his index finger from left to right.*) No amount of money can buy the level of respect, prestige, or honor that this show will bring to Nigeria, in particular, and Africa, in general! (*Quickly*) It will be huge! Of inestimable value to our dear country. If the critics are sincere that our government need not guarantee the fight, then they should promptly commence their own campaign to ensure a full house for the fight! (*Leaning forward*) Let us bring this epic match—Tiger versus Fullmer III—to our country, Nigeria! (*The crowd, which now has more than doubled in size, excitedly applauds the spokesperson and begins chanting, while waving fists in the air. They march through the street of Lagos chanting*)

CROWD, *chanting.* Tiga must fight at home! Fight at home! Tiga must fight at home! Fight at home!

(*As they march, hundreds more join in. The "Fight-at-Home" march quickly spreads to parts of the country*)

SCENE FIVE

ABIGAIL. My husband, the great Dick Tiger, took time from his training regimen to receive the 1962 Fighter-of-the-Year award, amidst the upheaval about the hosting site for the fight between him and Fullmer. The Fighter-of-the-Year award is given to a boxer who, during the year, by his conduct and boxing prowess, has merited the esteem of fight fans and the viewing public. At the reception to celebrate this feat, Chief S.O. Adebo, Nigeria's ambassador to the United Nations, was on hand to witness the ceremony.

He seized upon the occasion to make a plea.

*Chief Simeon Adebo addressing guests at a
banquet held in honor of Dick Tiger.*

CHIEF S. O. ADEBO, *standing*. It is indeed a pleasure and
an honor for me to be here today to mark an important
milestone in my friend, Dick Tiger's life. We are indeed
proud of him and wish him many more successes (*pauses*) His
life story teaches us to reach for the stars in the skies and
grab them! I am excited for him. (*Clearing his throat.*) We,
the Nigerians, have had two world champions, but neither
has boxed as champion in his homeland (*Pauses*). Here in
the United States, there are championship fights all the time.
How could one convince forty million Nigerians that that
was right? We would love to have Dick Tiger fight before his
people in Nigeria. Don't you think that we are entitled to host
the world championship, since one of our sons is a principal
player in the impending tussle to grab the Middleweight

Championship belt? We want Dick Tiger to fight for us, in our country of Nigeria while he is still champion. I, on behalf of the Nigerian people, implore the boxing officials to consider a Tiger versus Fullmer fight in Nigeria. Thank you. (*He sits.*)

DICK TIGER, *smiling broadly, stands.* Thank you very much, Your Excellency, Chief Adebo. (*Brief pause*) First of all, I am extremely honored by this recognition, and I thank very much the various boxing associations that helped to make it possible for me to receive this award. My manager, Jersey Jones, and my trainer, Jimmy August, I thank you specially, and I know that I couldn't have done it without your stellar guidance and support. (*Clearing his throat.*) I receive this award on behalf of the Nigerian people and the whole of Africa! (*Pause*) I know that our friends in the boxing business will do right by us. I think the time to give Nigeria and Black Africa the chance to host a world boxing championship is now! (*Pauses*) As the Honorable Chief Adebo has said, (*Giving great weight to each word.*) Nigeria has produced two world champions; it will be in keeping with the spirit of true sportsmanship to permit the upcoming world middleweight championship match between Gene Fullmer and me to be hosted in Nigeria, West Africa. (*Guests applaud.*) I also use this golden opportunity to extend an invitation to all of you seated here. Come see Nigeria! The weather is warm, the people are friendly, and we cook our meats (*mumbles*) not medium rare, but well-done! (*There's a smatter of giggling.*) Thank you. (*He takes his seat.*)

SCENE SIX

ABIGAIL. Jersey Jones had been invited to the United Nations by Their Excellencies, Chief Adebo, the Nigerian ambassador to the UN, and Chief J. M. Udochi, the Nigerian ambassador to the United States. At the meeting, he deliberated, and reached a settlement with the two diplomats as to the ramifications of hosting a world-championship match in Nigeria.

(*In Ambassador Adebo's office at the United Nations Building*)

CHIEF ADEBO and CHIEF UDOCHI, *upon Jersey's entrance, simultaneously*. Good morning, Mr. Jones. (*They stand, shake hands, and offer him a seat.*)

JERSEY JONES. Good morning, Your Excellencies, Chief Udochi and Chief Adebo.

CHIEF UDOCHI. Mr. Jones, thanks for seeing us on such short notice. We appreciate you meeting with us.

CHIEF ADEBO. Yes, the meeting is of gross importance, not just to Nigeria, but to Africa, and, if I may add, the sport of boxing.

CHIEF UDOCHI, *eagerly*. We want the third fight between Dick Tiger and Gene Fullmer to be held in Nigeria.

JERSEY JONES, *feeling a lump in his throat, shifts in his seat*. I'm sure that it'd be nice to have Dick box before his people in his home country of Nigeria. However, there are a lot of (*pauses*) ramifications to be explored and considered.

CHIEF ADEBO, *quickly*. Let's hear them, Mr. Jones.

JERSEY JONES, *fidgeting with his tie*. Boxing is a very popular sport right now, and we now have huge turnouts, especially in fights like the upcoming Tiger-versus-Fullmer fight. We are expecting to seat tens of thousands of spectators for gate receipts totaling over one hundred thousand dollars.

CHIEF ADEBO, *unfazed*. Nigeria can boast of a world-class stadium that can seat up to sixty thousand persons for football, even more for boxing.

JERSEY JONES, *feeling choked, he loosens his tie.* I can't remember when a boxing match was last held in Africa, but I know that a world-championship fight of such depth would require a capable boxing promoter to handle the rigors, challenges, and logistics inherent to such a highly billed match.

CHIEF ADEBO, *assuredly.* But we can bring in the best of them all— Jack Solomons of London. (*Jersey is visibly impressed.*) He is a dear friend of ours and the guru of boxing promotions!

JERSEY JONES, *nodding in approval.* Oh, yes, he is a magus in boxing promotions.

CHIEF UDOCHI, *interjecting.* We already have a world-champion boxer, in the person of Hogan Bassey (*Pause*) You know him, Mr. Jones? He is Nigeria's first world boxing champion.

JERSEY JONES. Of course, I know Hogan. I knew Hogan before I knew Tiger. I used to help coach him when he was campaigning for the world featherweight championship.

CHIEF UDOCHI. Great. Hogan Bassey is a capable hand and will complement Jack in this undertaking. Bassey already knows the business of boxing, and he is familiar with the Nigerian landscape and its people. He will assist Mr. Solomons in this venture.

JERSEY JONES, *shifting his eyes from side to side, feeling like a fish out of water.* A match of this scope will require a lot of capital to fund it. (*Quickly*) And we already have three different boxing promoters who have bid huge sums—more than a hundred thousand dollars—to host the fight here in America or London.

CHIEF ADEBO, *adjusting his agbada.* Funding is not going to be the bone of contention in this matter at all. The entire citizenry of the Republic of Nigeria wants this fight to happen in Nigeria. (*Pause. Jersey drops his gaze, looks up momentarily and drops it again.*) Seventy thousand pounds sterling, which is about two hundred thousand, has already been raised by various clubs and organizations in Nigeria. (*Nodding*) I am sure that the Nigerian government would not mind putting a guarantee on this fight. (*Saying each word slowly.*) We, the over forty million people of Nigeria, deliriously desire to see our son, Dick Tiger, fight Gene Fullmer in Nigeria this year while he is still the world champion.

JERSEY JONES, *looks up, sharply, just in time to interrupt a knowing glance between the two diplomats. Words die away on his lips and unable to hide a guilty grin, let's out a stifled laugh, and gently gets up from his seat.* I have heard your requests. (*Clearing his throat*) I will go back and pour over the ramifications with my partners. (*Stretching out his hand*) It's been a pleasure. (*They shake hands.*) Thank you.

BOTH CHIEFS. Thank You, Mr. Jones.

CHIEF ADEBO. Please keep us posted every step of the way.

JERSEY JONES. Will do. Good-bye. (*He exits*)

Scene Seven

ABIGAIL. Outside, Jersey ponders the possible implications of his meeting with the Nigerian dignitaries.

(Near the United Nations Building)

JERSEY JONES, *walking slowly, pensively.* Wow! What just happened in there? Do these people really think that they are capable of absorbing the financial, logistical, and other demands involved in hosting a world-championship event? (*Rolling his eyes.*) What in Africa? (*Pushing out his lips*) There are no two ways about it. (*Mumbles*) All aspects have to be carefully and thoroughly considered. I don't care whether it'd please Dick or not. (*Scratching his head*) It all boils down to which camp could withstand the financial and logistical toll that it'd take to host a world championship of this magnitude—the Nigerians, or Rothschild, or Rhodes? (*He halts abruptly, squeezing both eyes almost to a close.*) This bout may be of historical importance! (*Quickly*) Africa—Black Africa, anyway—has never hosted a world-championship bout! (*Eyes glistening*) History is in the making here. (*He begins rubbing his hands, slowly.*) They *did* say that they already have a guarantee (*Pauses*) My fighter, Dick Tiger, is the principal player in the fight; we are going to make history! (*Hopeful*) I, Wilfred Jersey Jones, am to be part of history—in faraway Africa? (*Pause.*) Okay, Tigerrr. (*Vigorously shaking his head*) I'd have to put things gently across to Norman and Co. (*Adjusting his trousers, he darts his eyes there and about.*) Nigeria, here we come!

SCENE EIGHT

ABIGAIL. Jersey Jones met with sports executives and promoters vying for the chance to showcase the Tiger-versus-Fullmer fight. When he informed them that they were out of the running, they began to loosen their grips but not without rancor.

(*In Jones's office*)

JERSEY JONES, *turning toward his office entrance, he gets up as he sees his guests arriving. Neil Rhodes, Norman Rothschild, and a British boxing promoter, Harry Levine, walk in. He shakes hands with them.* Hi, guys. (*Motioning them toward chairs*) Please make yourselves comfortable.

RHODES, *a bald-headed, cigar-chomping sports promoter*. How ya doin', Jersey?

JERSEY JONES. Just fine, thanks.

ROTHSCHILD and LEVINE, *simultaneously*. Hi, Jersey.

LEVINE, *quickly*. How do you do?

JERSEY JONES, *abruptly*. Gentlemen, you are welcome. (*Pause.*) As you know, a lot of interest has been generated by the upcoming match between Dick Tiger and Gene Fullmer. (*They nod in agreement, and he folds his hands around his body.*) I do declare that I am personally flabbergasted by the progression of events since both fighters fought to a draw in Las Vegas (*Taking a deep breath.*). There had been a question of who will do the promotions for the fight, as well as where to host the third bout—

ROTHSCHILD, *interjecting*. You know that we are the best of all the boxing promoters out there an—

LEVINE, *exploding*. Pure rubbish! I beg your pardon, Mr. Rothschild, but my outfit successfully promoted and hosted world-championship matches years before you guys ever thought of dabbling into the bloody business!

ROTHSCHILD. Yeah, sure! But your company seems to be losing its touch with each passing year, just as quickly as it takes a snake to shed old skin! (*Quickly*) It's over for you guys!

LEVINE, *increasingly agitated*. How dare y—

JERSEY JONES, *interjecting*. Gentlemen! Please, stop the rancor! I called you here (*mumbling*) simply to thank you for your interest in hosting the Tiger-versus-Fullmer fight.

RHODES, *indignantly*. What are you saying, Jersey? (*Miffed*) I thought we'd agreed that you wouldn't agree on anything! Without first consulting my office!

JERSEY JONES, *sternly*. I did not agree to any such stipulations. You casually asked me to not engage in any commitments regarding a hosting site for the match, without first consulting you (*stressed*) We did not reach any formal agreement.

RHODES, *suspiciously*. So, which company is going to host the match?

JERSEY JONES, *speaking very fast*. The Nigerian government is going to host the fight in their country of Nigeria.

ROTHSCHILD, *stunned*. What the dawggone heck!

JERSEY JONES, *there's silence; Jersey regrettably*. It's been a tough call, (*pause*) more like having a monkey on my back!

ROTHSCHILD, *maliciously*. When was this agreement made?

JERSEY JONES. In the past week. I met with the dignitaries of that government, and they basically informed me that they have a guarantee for up to two hundred thousand dollars to host the event.

RHODES, *lighting a cigar*. What the hell do you know about Nigeria? (*Taking a generous puff of his cigar.*) Do you have the agreement in writing? (*Gazing intently.*) 'Cause I know a bit about the Nigerian people (*pauses*) if it's not in writing and sealed in blood, then you'd have more than a monkey on your back. (*Taking another deep puff.*) You'd have some freakin' gorillas on your freakin' back! (*They cackle.*)

JERSEY JONES, *feeling flustered*. Gentlemen—

LEVINE. Who's bloody promoting this fight, hah?

JERSEY JONES, *wearily, giving great weight to each word.* The Nigerian government will be hosting the match in Nigeria. The guarantee for the match has been set at two hundred thousand dollars, and Jack Solomons of London has been picked to promote the match.

LEVINE, *astonished.* That's ace! He's probably the best in the business! If he's really pitted to promote the Tiger-Fullmer fight, then it's sure to be a grand showcase!

JONES. Yeah (*mumbling*) they're making all kinds of arrangements a—

(*Phone rings*)

JERSEY JONES. Excuse me. (*Picking up*) Hello.

CHIEF JMJ. Hello, Jersey, how are you?

JERSEY JONES. Chief Johnson, how are you?

CHIEF JMJ. I'm fine, Jersey. Listen, we have the guarantee to host the match in Nigeria. I'd like to know when you can get together with Mr. Jensen and Jack Solomons to view the facilities of the venue and discuss the match in further detail.

JERSEY JONES, *repeating Chief Johnson's words, and eyeing his guests.* You already have the guarantee to host the match in Nigeria. Very well, I'll try to get a hold of Jensen. You might want to put a call through to Jack Solomons in London.

CHIEF JMJ, All right, and hopefully we will see you guys in Nigeria before the end of the month.

JERSEY JONES. Okay, we'll see you then, Chief. (*He hangs up the phone.*)

ROTHSCHILD, *they are silent for ages, and then he shoots up from his seat with Rhodes in tow.* Okay Jersey, good luck on the show.

RHODES. Yeah (*pauses*) good luck, and we'll see ya later. (*They exit.*)

JERSEY JONES. Thanks, guys. See you.

LEVINE, *straightening himself.* Well Jersey, all the best, and be careful over there. Good luck. (*He leaves.*)

JONES. Thank you. (*Wiping anxious sweat off his face and neck, he picks up the phone to call Jack Solomons in London.*)

Scene Nine

ABIGAIL. Chief JMJ had managed to secure a promise of a two-hundred-thousand-dollar guarantee from the Nigerian government, including the use of the world-class facilities of the Liberty Stadium in Ibadan, as a venue for the upcoming match. Jersey consulted with my husband, Dick Tiger and Jimmy August about the latest developments.

(*Dick Tiger and Jimmy August meet in Jersey's office.*)

JERSEY JONES, *lamenting.* All my life I had hoped for the chance to manage a world champion, but I never thought that it would task me so much, turn me into an international incident.

DICK TIGER and JIMMY AUGUST, *confused.* What?

DICK TIGER, What do you mean by that?

JERSEY JONES, *moving about restlessly.* The Nigerian dignitaries figured that since my fighter, Dick Tiger, is a Nigerian, it was literally a done deal that the return match would be held in Nigeria. (*Wiping his face.*) And it looks like they've got it.

DICK TIGER. Good job, Jersey! You will not regret it.

JONES, *waving his hand.* Wait, I gave them a lot of reasons why the bout shouldn't be held in Nigeria, but (*Groaning*) they answered them all.

DICK TIGER. So, what is the problem? Did they tell you anything about the amount of money raised for the event?

JERSEY JONES. They informed me that they had already raised seventy thousand pounds, which is about two hundred thousand dollars, from various clubs and organizations in Nigeria.

DICK TIGER, *impressed.* Great! (*Pauses*) You've got to admit that's super encouraging. That's well over what the other promoters are offering!

JIMMY AUGUST. Yeah!

JERSEY JONES, *confidentially to Tiger.* You'd be getting a hundred thousand, and Fullmer will get sixty thousand.

(*Phone rings.*)

JERSEY JONES. One moment please, it's probably the chief. (*Picking up.*) Hello.

CHIEF JMJ. Jersey, how are you?

JERSEY JONES. I'm fine, Chief Johnson. How are you?

CHIEF JMJ. Fine, Jersey. Just to let you know that a British gentleman, Jack Hart, has been billed to referee the fight in Ibadan, Nigeria. We hear that he is one of the best in his field.

JERSEY JONES. Oh, great!

CHIEF JMJ. Have you spoken to Solomons and Jensen?

JERSEY JONES. I have been in touch with Solomons, but I'm yet to get ahold of Jensen. I'll definitely call him again first thing tomorrow morning.

CHIEF JMJ. Good. Keep me posted.

JERSEY JONES. I sure will, Chief. (*He hangs up the phone and continues his discourse with Tiger and Jimmy August.*)

Scene Ten

ABIGAIL. Jersey Jones called Marv Jensen to report on developments in the impending world middleweight boxing championship. Jensen was apprehensive at first, but realizing that their refusal could cost Fullmer his chances at the world title, he conceded. An agreement was reached concerning the date of arrival in Nigeria.

(*In Marv Jensen's office*)

MARV JENSEN, *phone rings; he picks up.* Hello!

JERSEY JONES. Hi, Marv. How are you doin'?

MARV JENSEN. Just fine. (*Anxiously.*) What's the latest news about the fight? I heard through the grapevine that they're considering hosting it (pauses) in Africa?

JERSEY JONES, *clearing his throat*. Mmm, yeah. The guarantees have been met, and they have a site mapped out for the fight already.

MARV JENSEN, *voice trailing*. I would have preferred another site other than Tiger's home country (*Motioning a hand in surrender.*), but Dick is the champion, and you guys are entitled to call the shots.

JERSEY JONES. Yeah, that is the situation at the moment. Arrangements have already been concluded. (*Slightly taunting*) But if you guys are not interested, Joey Giardello has been agitating for a crack at the title. (*Quickly*) We have been invited by Minister Johnson to come to Nigeria to take a tour of the venue, to decide if it'd be of standard to host an event of such magnitude.

MARV JENSEN, *quickly*. Well, uh, when d'ya think we should head out there?

JERSEY JONES. The minister suggested the end of the month, but if you want to get there earlier, Jack Solomons, who's been contracted to promote the event, would not mind leaving middle of the month.

MARV JENSEN. Superb! (*Surprised*) Solomons is promoting? Wow, they are pulling out all the stops at their disposal to ensure that this fight is truly an epic match. With that said, I think that I'd rather we leave at the end of the month.

JERSEY JONES. It's a deal then. I'll inform Solomons to plan to converge in Nigeria at the end of the month.

MARV JENSEN. Thank you, Jersey. I think it should be all right. Besides, we were very impressed by the Nigerian people who represented that nation at the first two bouts.

JERSEY JONES. See you in Nigeria! (*He hangs up the phone.*)

Act Eight

SCENE ONE

DICK TIGER SR. Jersey Jones arrived in Nigeria on June 27, along with Marv Jensen, Jack Solomons, and Bobby Diamond. Chief Johnson is on hand with some members of his cabinet to welcome them and give them a tour of the Liberty Stadium in Ibadan, the proposed site of the bout. Ibadan is one of the oldest cities in Africa and is also a sort of cradle of civilization in West Africa. Founded in the early nineteenth century, it is located in Southwestern Nigeria and serves as the seat of government in the western region. Home to the oldest university in Nigeria and the first television station in Africa (NTA Ibadan), Ibadan is also densely populated because of its reputation as a commercial hub of the western region. The Liberty Stadium, the first stadium in Africa and the venue of the first-ever world boxing championship match in Africa, is situated in Ibadan.

(*At Lagos International Airport*)

CHIEF JMJ, *smiling broadly and coming toward his guests with outstretched hands.* Jersey! Jack! Bobby! Marv! You are all welcome to our beautiful, sunny country of Nigeria.

JACK SOLOMONS, *jokingly.* I hear it rains a lot down here too!

(*Solomons is a magus in boxing. He is very businesslike, a tough bargainer, resourceful, and efficient.*)

CHIEF JMJ, *laughing*. Don't believe everything you hear, Jack. Here (*Pointing to a group of men.*), these gentlemen are from my Ministry: Mr. Talade, Mr. Williams, and Mr. Okoro. They will be accompanying us to the site.

SOLOMONS, JONES, JENSON, and DIAMOND, *together*. Hello! (*They shake hands with each other.*)

JERSEY JONES, *smiling mischievously*. I remember Mr. Talade from the party at the Mark Hopkins Club in San Fran; he was one of the delegates that came with you (*Motioning to Chief JMJ*) to the first fight. (*To Mr. Talade.*) Where's Mr. Wulite?

MR. TALADE, *speaking very fast*. He's in town, Sir.

CHIEF JMJ, *recalling*. Oh, yes, they were part of our entourage. (*Quickly*) You guys must be famished. Do you care for some refreshments?

BOBBY DIAMOND and JERSEY JONES. No.

JACK SOLOMONS. Nah, maybe later.

MARV JENSEN. Yeah, let's first get a look at the proposed site!

CHIEF JMJ. Sure, let's go!

SCENE TWO

DICK TIGER SR. All parties approved of the site as a world-class standard gymnasium, suitable to hold an international competition. When Solomons produced a detailed estimate of the envisaged costs, the numbers do not match earlier quotes. Emotions had run high amongst certain factions of the Nigerian public with the earlier projection. However, with mounting pressure from some of the local press and the general public, responsive political leaders agreed to underwrite the entire event with Hogan Bassey listed as co-promoter for the event.

(*At the Liberty Stadium, they stroll around, inspecting facilities.*)

JACK SOLOMONS, *nodding affirmatively.* This is more than I had expected. (*Smiling faintly, he rubs his hands.*) I am very impressed with the standard of the facilities at this stadium.

JERSEY JONES. Oh, Chiefs Adebo and Udochi earlier attested to its grandeur when I met with them in New York.

MARV JENSEN. Marvelous. (*Pointing.*) The boxing ring is of world class standard, and the bleachers should be able to fit about (*mumbles)* forty thousand spectators, comfortably.

CHIEF JMJ, *proudly.* It can hold up to fifty thousand people, and the facilities are world class!

JACK SOLOMONS, *patiently pulls some papers from his briefcase and hands them to JMJ.* Here, Chief. It's a detailed estimate of the costs for hosting the championship bout.

CHIEF JMJ, *shocked.* Mr. Solomons, this estimate is too high! It's eighty thousand more than was originally budgeted for. I'm not sure if we can do more than the earlier amount of two hundred thousand. (*Anxious, he motions to his escorts. They huddle over to deliberate on Jack Solomons's latest quote for the meet)*

JACK SOLOMONS, *surprised.* Chief Johnson, this show could possibly rank as one of the greatest shows on earth! Hasn't that occurred to you? Instead of brooding over possible losses, I think the whole country should focus on winning! After all, Nigeria's Dick Tiger, the undisputed world middleweight boxing champion, is one of the principal players.

CHIEF JMJ, *wearily.* Mr. Solomons, the hosting of the upcoming event has generated a lot of controversy in this country, with a percentage of the population against the fight, branding it a "misguided sense of national priorities," while a majority of the people want the fight to happen here in Nigeria. I'm all tied up in knots, 'cause I, too, as the sports minister in this country, would like to fulfill the wishes of millions of Nigerians to see our own world-champion boxer, Dick Tiger, box in his own country, before his countrymen.

JACK SOLOMONS, *calmly.* When we were first asked to host this event, we had no intention of putting it on. We wondered where, for Pete's sake, in Nigeria, are they going to put on a world-championship fight? But we figured we'd just show the courtesy of talking to you guys. So, lo and behold, we come to Ibadan, and we find that you guys have got as nice a stadium as you could find anywhere in the world! And you are making all these preparations. (*Shaking his head in amazement.*) Gor blimey, I cannot get out of it. (*Pause*) I think that you are making a smart move in agreeing to host this epochal event. (*Handing a pen to Chief Johnson.*) As soon as this is sealed with your signature, Chief Johnson, we will set the match meet for July 13.

CHIEF JMJ, *taking the pen.* It is going to be a historic event (*Pause.*) and in the middle of the rainy season, huh?

JACK SOLOMONS, *quickly.* There's no better time than now. We will watch the weather, and if postponements have to happen, then we'll make them, until we get favorable weather.

CHIEF JMJ, *apologetically.* Though the promotion of professional sports is not the responsibility of a government, we felt that the yearning of our countrymen and women to see Tiger should be encouraged. We are not taking on the role of promoters; all we are doing is guaranteeing the sale of all the tickets. (*Adjusting his agbada, then his specs.*) If all tickets are not sold, the government would ensure a full house by giving the unsold tickets to schools, orphanages, and other charities. (*He signs and hands the papers to Mr. Solomons.*) C'mon, gentlemen, let's head to the Eko Holiday Inn restaurant!

Scene Three

DICK TIGER SR. Oblivious of the fight-fever looming in my country, I commenced vigorous training for the match at New York's Catholic Youth Association Gym. I was perturbed, however, by Fullmer's seemingly nonchalant disposition toward the upcoming fight in Nigeria.

JIMMY AUGUST. Time out, Tiger. Let's take a break; you've been sparring for much longer than the required time. (*He motions for the sparring partner to leave.*) We have to ration out the amount of strength that you expend at one time during training, so that you don't burn out.

DICK TIGER, *skipping ropes.* Jimmy, I can handle it. I'd know when I'd need to take a break.

JIMMY AUGUST. C'mon, Dick, you'd need to take five, after exactly five minutes. If you want to beat Fullmer by a knockout, then you need to play by the rules. You cannot expend all your energy in the training sessions.

(*After five minutes, Dick drops the ropes and picks up a mop to clean the sweat spilled all over the gym*)

JIMMY AUGUST. That's not your job, Tiger! Take it easy.

DICK TIGER, *quickly*. Where's Jersey? He hasn't given any updates on the progression of arrangements for the fighters.

JIMMY AUGUST, *confused*. Wh…what d'ya mean, Tiger?

DICK TIGER, *snapping*. Well, we haven't heard anything about whether Fullmer is training or whether he's going to back out of the fight or—

JIMMY AUGUST, Tiger, (*mumbles*) stop. You are worrying too much about things. Fullmer is going to face you again in the ring in Nigeria. He needs the fight as much as you, in order to determine who the undisputed middleweight boxing champion of the world will be!

DICK TIGER, *gently hitting his chest*. I'm going to be the undisputed middleweight champion when I box him before my people in Nigeria.

JIMMY AUGUST, I know you'll win. (*Pause*) Just learn to take it easy on yourself.

Scene Four

DICK TIGER SR. Jersey Jones was back in the United States, and he called me to announce the date of the match. I decided to leave for Nigeria at the end of June to continue with my training for the bout.

DICK TIGER, *phone rings and he picks up*. Hello.

JERSEY JONES, Hi, Tiger. How's the training coming along?

DICK TIGER, Just fine. When did you return?

JERSEY JONES, Yesterday evening. Plans are in full swing now. We met with Chief Johnson upon our arrival as planned, and he took us on an exhaustive tour of the facilities.

DICK TIGER. How was it?

JERSEY JONES. Not bad at all. Actually, we were amazed by what we saw in Africa, (*feeling overwhelmed*) the people, culture—

DICK TIGER. What about the site, Jersey?

JERSEY JONES. It was magnificent, a full-fledged, functioning world-class stadium! I did not think they had things like that in Africa.

DICK TIGER. Well, there's a lot the Western world doesn't know about Nigeria or Africa. The upcoming Dick Tiger–Gene Fullmer fight will help to erase some of the misgivings.

JERSEY JONES. I hope so, Tiger. I certainly wish your people well. Nice people. The ticket prices will range from $1.47 to $29.40 a piece for ringside seats.

DICK TIGER. When is the date?

JERSEY JONES. July 13 is the date we have chosen.

DICK TIGER. That's in the middle of the rainy season over there! Let's hope the rains will give way on that day.

JERSEY JONES. Solomons said that if the rains disrupt proceedings there, we would just keep shifting dates until it is conducive for the fighters and the people. The move now is to get those tickets into the hands of the Nigerian people. Chief Johnson has predicted a full stadium.

DICK TIGER. With that in mind, at the end of June, I will head out to Nigeria with Jimmy in order to continue training.

JERSEY JONES. That sounds practical, Tiger.

DICK TIGER. See you later. (*He hangs up the phone.*)

JERSEY JONES. See you.

SCENE FIVE

DICK TIGER SR. The date for the fight was moved once again from July 13 to July 27, 1963. Fullmer's camp had on June 21, reported that Fullmer had sprained his ankle while training, and as a result requested the fight be moved back. The postponement did not sit well with me, and especially the Nigerian people. There was a general outcry in the press and among the Nigerian citizenry. Amid the uncertainties looming, some welcome news arrived.

(*At the gym, in New York*)

JERSEY JONES, *entering the gym, he waves to Tiger and Jimmy.* Hi, guys. (*Hesitating.*) I've got good news and bad news.

JIMMY AUGUST, *flushed*. Oh boy! What is it now?

JERSEY JONES. Fullmer sprained his ankle while training; therefore, the fight has been reset for July 27.

DICK TIGER. Do you think that he's going to be able to defend in the fight?

JERSEY JONES. Of course, he will. They said that he'd need just about two weeks to nurse the sore ankle. I know one thing:

The Nigerian public is not going to be too happy about this latest development.

DICK TIGER. Very well. We will still leave for Nigeria on June 24, as earlier planned. I have a lot more sparring and training to do.

JERSEY JONES. Go ahead with whatever plans you've made, Tiger. I know your work ethic and the nature of your training regimen. (*Beaming.*) The whole world knows it too! Congratulations, Dick, on being one of the honorees to receive the distinguished award of Commander of the British Order from Her Majesty Queen Elizabeth! (*Slight pause.*) It's for your remarkable contributions to the sport of boxing.

JIMMY AUGUST. Congratulations, Tiger! I'm so proud of you.

DICK TIGER, *bashfully.* That is very nice. Thank you. (*With a soft smile.*) I couldn't have done it without you guys. Thank you so much, and see you in Nigeria!

Act Nine

SCENE ONE

DICK TIGER SR. My trainer and I arrived in Nigeria on June 24 to a rousing welcome at Ikeja Airport in Lagos. People came in droves to await my arrival, and after briefly exchanging pleasantries with the crowd, I was whisked off in a motorcade. I touched base first with my good friend and co-promoter of the event, Hogan Bassey, before heading to my training site at the Abalti Army Barracks to inspect the reconstruction underway.

(*At Hogan Bassey's residence in Lagos*)

HOGAN BASSEY, *elated, arms outstretched.* Tiga! Tiga! (*They embrace.*) You are still looking good and well-conditioned. (*As he's looking him over, Tiger playfully flexes his muscles.*) No! Fullmer doesn't have a chance here! (*They laugh.*)

DICK TIGER. How are you, Bassey? You don't look bad yourself. (*Looking around.*) Where is Madam? Where are the kiddies?

HOGAN BASSEY. Please, sit down. She hurried to the market to get some foodstuff to prepare some scrumptious *Edi kai kong* soup for you!

DICK TIGER. C'mon, she shouldn't have. I just wanted to get a whiff of you and your family before heading to my training site at the army barracks. I really cannot tarry here long. Even as we speak, loads of materials for constructing a boxing ring at the site are right now making their way all the way from New York to the barracks. (*Pause.*) Do you mind coming along?

HOGAN BASSEY. Not a problem, my friend. (*Throwing on his agbada.*) Let's go!

Scene Two

DICK TIGER SR. Hogan Bassey and I met up with Jimmy August at the site. We conversed about some current events while overseeing the construction. Satisfied with the progression of the work, we decided to return to Hogan's home to have dinner.

(*At Abalti Barracks*)

DICK TIGER. You do know the fight has been reset for July 27, eh?

HOGAN BASSEY. Yes, Solomons kept me up on that development. That is just a shame. (*Waving his hands at his sides.*) The press and the public don't buy the story. They think Fullmer is either trying to evade the duel or thinks Africa is filled with diseases and barbarians.

DICK TIGER, *sternly*. The earlier his foot heals, the better for all of us.

HOGAN BASSEY, *shaking his head in amazement*. Your fight with Fullmer has really become a national obsession and has for some time been a focal point of debates on the floor of the parliament. (*Crossing his arms.*) And to think that the "big show" is slated to happen in the thick of the rainy season! Heavens help us! (*Pause*) You know our irrepressible showman of a minister, Chief Johnson? He has announced that he is going to hire rain doctors to keep the rains at bay! (*They snicker.*)

DICK TIGER. Incredible! Does he believe they'd be able to hold Mother Nature? They tried that on the eve of the Nigerian Independence celebration, almost three years ago, and it didn't work (*Pauses*) Remember?

HOGAN BASSEY, *affirmatively.* Oh yes! (*Continuing the story.*) And despite the government's payment of $2,800 to the rain doctors, through the Oba of Lagos, Adele Adeniyi, to keep the rain from falling on Princess Alexandra who was representing Her Majesty Queen Elizabeth at the ceremony. (*Smirks*) What happened?

TIGER and BASSEY, *loudly.* She still got drenched to the bones! (*Both men bend over laughing.*)

DICK TIGER, *wiping sweat from his brow.* Incredible! Unbelievable! (*Pause*) But you know, the rain doctors may be able to more accurately forecast the weather, if only we can marry their method—the traditional method—with the modern approach, where satellite dishes and customized computers help in providing more accurate forecasts of the weather. Jus—

HOGAN BASSEY, *interjecting.* Just as it's done in the Western world, eh? We don't have anything like that, as yet. (*With a wave.*) But listen, the rain doctors in the eastern region are also clamoring for some notoriety.

TIGER, *incredulously.* No kidding! All the way from there? What are they asking for?

HOGAN BASSEY, Well, for them, it is about ensuring that the antics of the warring southern rain doctors in Lagos and Ibadan do not get in the way of an assurance of a rainless day for the big fight. (*Pause*) They have vowed to launch a series of incantations and chants and sacrifices to their god of rain to appease him (*mumbles*) uh, to restrain the rain in Ibadan for D-Day.

DICK TIGER, *solemnly*. Wow! I am touched by the gesture (*He takes off his homburg hat to wipe away sweat and puts it back on.*), but those are some of the die-hard superstitions that perpetuate the Western world's perception of Africa and Africans as uncivilized and barbaric. It's unfortunate.

HOGAN BASSEY, *nodding in agreement*. Here! Here! We can surely do better.

DICK TIGER, *walking toward Jimmy*. Hogan, remember my trainer, Jimmy August?

HOGAN BASSEY. Oh yes. How are you, sir?

JIMMY AUGUST. Just fine, Hogan, and you?

HOGAN BASSEY. Fine, thank you.

JIMMY AUGUST. The work here is not bad at all. (*Looking around.*) These structures can last forever!

DICK TIGER. I am very impressed by the work. We might even be able to use the facilities today.

JIMMY AUGUST. Dick, you just got off the plane! It was a long trip.

We will resume training tomorrow.

HOGAN BASSEY. Yeah, Dick. Let's go. My wife should have finished making dinner, and she doesn't like it when dinner is served late.

DICK TIGER. Well then, let's go. I'm not going to be the one to keep the madam waiting.

Scene Three

DICK TIGER SR. Marv Jensen was racked with guilt over the progression of the Dick Tiger–Gene Fullmer fight. He was burdened by a secret that he is keeping from the international press and the millions of Nigerian people frustrated by Fullmer's prevarications in the much-anticipated, first-ever world-championship bout to be hosted on African soil. For how long will he keep this secret? What ramifications will it have on the epochal event?

MARV JENSEN, *on the phone.* Hello, Gene. How is the training coming along?

GENE FULLMER, *animated.* As well as could be imagined, sir. Yeah, Milos, my sparring partner, is great too! The facilities are holding up great, too! (*Jokingly.*) What's your problem? (*Suddenly serious.*) How is she?

MARV JENSEN, *choking back tears.* She is not getting better, Gene. The doctors are running more tests in order to ascertain the nature of the illness. I'm sorry, Gene.

GENE FULLMER, *sympathetically.* Hey, it's all right—

MARV JENSEN. I feel horrible that I am inadvertently stalling your progress, because my life is in a hole right now! I am so sorry, Gene. You know that I would never knowingly hurt you.

GENE FULLMER, *emphatically*. It's nowhere near your fault, Marv. You didn't bring on your wife's illness. Please don't make me feel any worse than I already do. (*Pause*) Why... in faraway Nigeria, word is that I am regarded with utter contempt, as much as one would have for a rodent! (*Dismayed*) But the Lord God will vindicate me!

MARV JENSEN, *struggling with his emotions*. Gene, I could have one of my friends stand in for me. You need to go to Nigeria and resume your training for this big match.

GENE FULLMER. I am training here, too. We will wait it out, Marv. Besides, I would not be able to focus, wondering about her health and, (*Smiling*) your sanity.

MARV JENSEN, *choking back tears*. It looks like I will have to announce another postponement, Gene! It's that serious. (*Uncontrollably*) The press has gotten it all wrong! They think it's your fault, Gene (*in shock*) they think it's your fault that a whole country is frustrated! Oh, if only they knew—

GENE FULLMER, *softly*. Ssshhh, it's all right. God knows the heart. We will keep praying, and we will postpone (*Hesitating*) one more time. If after this one, she doesn't get better (*Hesitating*), then I would unleash Joey Giardello, who has been pathetically salivating for that chance to go fight Dick Tiger in Nigeria for the middleweight crown. (*Pause*) Don't worry about me. Take care of yourself and your wife.

MARV JENSEN. Bless you, Gene. (*He hangs up the phone.*)

SCENE FOUR

DICK TIGER SR. I promptly resumed training. Over five hundred of my fellow Nigerians converged daily to watch me train. The crowd proved a constant source of irritation for Jimmy August, as they shrieked with excitement at every punch I threw during the sparring sessions. Hogan Bassey and Bobby Diamond stopped by for a chat and with news of a possible second postponement. I was disappointed but not angry. I, however, readjusted my plans.

(*At Abalti Gym*)

JIMMY AUGUST, *scrutinizing Tiger's every move.* Move those feet quicker, faster! Keep it up, Tiger! Keep moving sharply! Jab and move! C'mon! Try to keep your eyes on your opponent's eyes! (*Loudly*) Keep your eyes on his eyes! It helps you gauge where he'll try to hit next! C'mon, move those legs quicker!

DICK TIGER, *putting his fists down momentarily.* But none of them has ever punched me with their eyes! I think focusing on their gloves would put me at a better advantage to gauge their reflexes. (*Hogan Bassey walks in with hefty, no-nonsense, wise-cracking Bobby Diamond.*)

BOBBY DIAMOND and HOGAN BASSEY. Hi, guys!

HOGAN BASSEY. I see training is going full blast!

JIMMY AUGUST. Hi there, Hogan, Bobby. (*They shake hands.*) Well, I'm amazed you made it through the stream of people at the entrance.

DICK TIGER, *catching his breath.* Hello, Hogan, Bobby.

BOBBY DIAMOND. Hi, Champ! I see you are not leaving any stones unturned in your training.

JIMMY AUGUST. Hey, Dick, I was just asking Hogan how they were able to maneuver their way through the pack of people outside.

HOGAN BASSEY, *striking a boxing pose.* They know I can box!

BOBBY DIAMOND, *jokingly.* Yeah, and I walked right behind him, for cover. (*They laugh.*)

JIMMY AUGUST, *gesturing.* The other day, I came with Bobby, but we missed the training session! We just couldn't squeeze through the melee of people! As if that wasn't bad enough, each time Dick threw a punch during the sparring sessions, they'd shriek, "Tiga! Tiga! Tiga!" (*Shaking his head.*) It was all so annoying! And would you believe (*mumbles*) this one here (*Pointing to Tiger*) appears, holding both hands above his head, like a politician campaigning for votes, saying, "Vote for me! Vote for me (*mumbles*) and I will promise you everything!" (*They laugh.*)

DICK TIGER. Oh, but Jimmy wasn't laughing. The next day, this man (*Pointing at Jimmy.*) went straight to the barracks and requested that an orderly be permanently stationed (*Punctuating*) at every corner of the site, including near the boxing ring!

HOGAN BASSEY, *looking around.* I see that.

BOBBY DIAMOND. Yeah! Totally!

DICK TIGER, *laughing.* It's all right with me. (*Beating his chest.*) As for me, I always come in through the less travelled entrance—through the back exit. (*Chuckling*)

JIMMY AUGUST. Look, I'm sure they didn't do it because of me; they knew that I was Tiger's trainer. They did it for Tiga!

BOBBY DIAMOND. There have been some memorable moments at this site, that's for sure. Remember the day when Chief Johnson was insisting that he would fight on the undercard and actually came in in just his shorts for a sparring session with Dick?

DICK TIGER, *tickled*. Oh yeah, and I sparred a few casual sessions with him.

BOBBY DIAMOND, *jokingly*. Mmm. Well, you say "casual," but he said (*Animatedly*) he only "played" with you, 'cause he did not want to harm you before the big fight!

(*They laugh*.)

DICK TIGER, *sarcastically*. Right! Of course!

HOGAN BASSEY, *proudly*. Congratulations, Tiga, on being one of the distinguished named to receive the British Medal of Honor from the Queen. You are amazing, my friend. You've come a long way, and I am so proud of you!

JIMMY AUGUST. Here! Here! He is amazing. He trains so hard! Even when I ask him to take a break, he doesn't want to. He gets restless and starts sweeping floors, washing his clothes, etc. He is remarkably humble too.

HOGAN BASSEY. Yes, that's why we love him!

BOBBY DIAMOND. Congratulations are very much in order, Tiger. Way to go!

DICK TIGER. Enough about me, you guys. Hogan, what's the latest news from Fullmer's camp? We haven't received any messages from Jersey lately. I'm sure he must be trying to reach us but hasn't been able to.

HOGAN BASSEY. Well, at a meeting the other day, Solomons said that it looks like Fullmer's foot is not healing fast enough, so, we'll see. (*Pause*) It's a despicable waiting game.

BOBBY DIAMOND. I personally don't believe their bloody excuses. They're tales, as far as I'm concerned.

DICK TIGER, *wearily* I...I miss my family, and with the uncertainties, I think I'll go see them in Aba and touch base with the rest of my folks in my village of Amaigbo.

JIMMY AUGUST. The break should be good for you, Dick.

HOGAN BASSEY. Yes, that sounds great. And please, do extend my warmest regards to Abigail and the children when you see them. I'll see you back here, soon.

DICK TIGER. Oh, yes, in one week's time.

SCENE FIVE

DICK TIGER SR. While in the East, I refused social invitations due to time constraints. Visitors bombarded my residence, but many were denied audience. I stayed mostly with my family, but later traveled to my village of Amaigbo to formally inform my kith and kin of my impending duel with Fullmer in Ibadan.

(*At Dick Tiger's residence in Aba*)

ABIGAIL, *with hands outstretched.* Di'm! Di'm! You are welcome. (*They hug, and the kids run into the room to embrace him.*)

DICK TIGER, *overcome by emotion, he holds his family to himself.* How are you? (*Pause.*) It's good to be home again.

ABIGAIL, *rubbing his back.* How are you, my dear husband? We are happy to have you home, (*Pause*) even if only briefly. (*They hug.*) The Good Lord is with you, and may He continue to preserve you. We love you, Di'm. (*She wipes his face.*)

Scene Six

Dick Tiger Sr. I arrived Amaigbo early Saturday morning. With news of my arrival came pandemonium. Though visibly moved by the reception, the impromptu praise, and the singing and dancing, I politely requested an audience with just the elders of the village. Pleasantries were exchanged with the brotherhood, and I partook of the traditional breaking of kola nuts with them. I judiciously informed them of my impending fight with Gene Fullmer in Ibadan.

(*At Amaigbo.*)

TOWN CRIER, *a frail-looking, gravel-voiced, elderly fellow, he is ringing a bell.* Umu Amaigbo! Chei! Our son, our brother, Dick Tiger, boxin' champon of tha world, the Lion Heart, will be amongst us today! (*Rings bell.*) Spread the word over the hilltops and below the fox holes. Dick Tiga, the grandest of all the tigas in Africa and Ashia, is in our midst! Be there at the village square to welcome him this afternoon! (*Exits, ringing bell.*)

(*At the village square, some women, while singing and dancing, usher Dick Tiger to a seat specially reserved for him.*)

(*Women Dancers enter singing.*)

WOMEN'S DANCING GROUP. Ihe Chukwu nyere anyi n'uwaa, owu ngozi, ihe onyere anyi n'uwaa, owu ngozi (Repeat two times.) Dicki Tiga of Nig-e-ria, owu ngozi, ihe onyere anyi n'uwaa, owu ngozi. (Repeat two times.) Kpakpandu onyere anyi n'uwaa, owu ngozi, ihe onyere anyi, n'uwaa, owu ngozi! (Repeat two times.) Chief JMJ of Nig-e-ria, owu ngozi, ihe Chukwu nyere anyi n'uwa, owu ngozi (Repeat two times.) Owelle Onitsha of Ni-ge-ria, owu ngozi, ihe Chukwu nyere anyi n'uwa, owu ngozi (Repeat two times.)

[Translated: "All God's gifts are blessings. Dick Tiger of Nigeria, is a blessing. All God's gifts are blessings. Stars in the sky are blessings; all God's gifts are blessings. Chief JMJ of Nigeria is a blessing. All God's gifts are blessings. Owelle Onitsha (AZikiwe) of Nigeria is a blessing. All God's gifts are blessings."]

DICK TIGER, *to the dancers.* Thank you. Thank you, dear sisters and mothers. You all look very beautiful. (*Grinning.*) I am very moved by your songs and the dancing. Thank you again. (*Pause.*) I am sorry that my stay here in the village will be brief, as I have to hurry and return to Lagos. I came with very special news, which I will grant the elders of our village the honor to pass on to you. Until I see you again in a few weeks, please remain blessed, and pray for me.

CROWD, *applauding and chanting.* Dike! Dike! Dike! (Brave one! Brave one! Brave one!)

TOWN CRIER. Our womens! You have heard Amaigbo's champon son, our broda, Dike Tiga! He is here in the village for a very short time and is happy about the way you welcoming him. (*Clearing his throat.*) Now, we ask that you leef us alone, so we can meet with him. The olders will inform you of Dike Tiga's special message later.

(*They sing and dance, as they exit.*)

DICK TIGER, *rising from his seat.* Umu nne'm nwoke, (My brothers) I am elated to be home to my beloved hometown of Amaigbo. (*Cheers.*) I know that you must have heard through the press and other people—maybe through the town crier, Cornelius (*They jeer.*)—but I wanted to come to you, personally, as a mark of the respect that I have for Amaigbo, to announce that yes, the news you heard is true. (*Cheering.*) I will be fighting America's Gene Fullmer for the third time, because I want to retain my current title as the middleweight boxing champion of the world. (*They burst into cheers and chanting of "Tiga! Tiga!" And he takes his seat.*)

NZE JOE UZOMA. You did well, our brother. Diki, *(Punctuating each word.)* for coming all this way to inform us about the upcoming great fight! *(Applause.)* Before we say anything else, we will first break kola nuts and ask Orisa to take charge. *(He lifts the kola nuts toward heaven.)* God will guide you!

CHORUS. Amen!

NZE JOE UZOMA. You will go, and you will win! *(Cheers. He pauses.)* Amaigbo will win! *(Cheers)* Nigeria will win *(Applause.)* As you take your leave from us, may Orisa guide you and your family.

CHORUS. Amen!

CHINAKA. May your ring opponent, Fulluma, also be safe.

CHORUS. Amen!

CHINAKA. He will come to our shores and do his work and leave safely. Protect him and his family too, Orisa *(Pauses)*, and give Dick Tiger, your son, our brother, the victory! *(There's a thunderous chorus of, "Amen!" Dick Tiger takes a bow. He exits after partaking of kola nuts with his kinsmen.)* We go now choose two peoples from our brothers here, make them represent us at Ibadan! Them go repot evry cheer, doge, and evry punch to all of us!

Scene Seven

DICK TIGER SR. I hurriedly returned to Aba the next day, and traveled back to Lagos on Monday. While in Aba, I insisted, once again, on not receiving visitors in the very limited time before my return to Lagos to resume training.

(*At Dick Tiger's Lodge in Aba.*)

ABIGAIL. I hope your meeting with the elders went well.

DICK TIGER. Yes, it did. (*Pausing*) It was soothing for my soul to be with them at that gathering; I am more at peace knowing that I have the blessing of my kinsmen to move forward with this fight.

ABIGAIL. You have my blessing, too. You have the blessings of millions of people in Nigeria, Africa, and the world! It shall be well with you. (*Pause*) Now, let's get some sleep. Remember, you have another long trip tomorrow.

DICK TIGER. Good night, my darling wife.

Act Ten

Scene One

DICK TIGER SR. With the news of a second postponement of the fight, the national press reloaded their arsenal for a media assault on Gene Fullmer and his camp. Said one paper, "FULLMER DODGES, AGAIN!" Another editorialized, "IF FULLMER CAN'T TAKE IT, HE SHOULD LEAVE IT!" Solomons and Chief Johnson embarked on "damage control" in order to ensure that ticket sales for the impending fight were not egregiously impacted.

(*Bobby Diamond and Jack Solomons at a café*)

BOBBY DIAMOND, *holding up a newspaper headline about Fullmer's equivocations.* Look at that! Don't Fullmer and his camp realize that everybody in Nigeria and the world has realized that their claim of a sore foot is yellow? They are trying to mislead the public into believing that Fullmer's reasons for yet another delay is genuine? No! They are covering up for Fullmer's fears of facing Tiger in the ring, if you ask me.

JACK SOLOMONS. Bobby, let's take it easy, they could be telling the truth. Actually, I just learned that Joseph Palmer, the American ambassador to Nigeria, had received a telegram from Fullmer's camp confirming that they will be arriving Nigeria on July 27.

BOBBY DIAMOND, *irritated.* See what I mean? Talk about a breach of protocol; now, why could they not inform you directly, as the chief promoter of the event? Or they could have called Tiger's camp. Jersey is still in the US awaiting more concrete news from Fullmer's camp. (*Animated*) Now tell me, what does an ambassador have to do with a boxing championship event? Fullmer is yellow! I say he is covering up and misleading the public.

(*A reporter walks in.*)

REPORTER, *to Solomons.* Good morning, sirs. I hope that you are finding your stay in Nigeria pleasurable.

JACK SOLOMONS, *clearing his throat.* It is a beautiful country, but you know that we are not here on vacation. We are here to put on one of the greatest shows on earth!

REPORTER, *eyes gleaming.* Yes, the Tiger versus Fullmer fight! (*Adjusting his microphone.*) Why did you decide to host in Nigeria, considering that she is only a new nation, with barely three years of independence after almost one hundred years of colonial rule?

JACK SOLOMONS. World-title fights are held all the time in America and in Britain, so we thought Nigeria, having produced two world champions, is deserving of the chance to host a world-championship fight.

REPORTER. Mr. Solomons, what do you think about Fullmer's latest claim about his injuries?

JACK SOLOMONS. Oh, it's just one of those kinds of bruises that are slow healing, but Fullmer is excited about the bout and has completed arrangements to be in the country before the end of July for a fight date on August 10.

BOBBY DIAMOND, *interjecting*. That's if he doesn't concoct another story to delay the bout. Look, the Nigerian public has already asserted through the press that Fullmer is suffering from "yellow fever." (*Indignantly*) We know that it is not of the kind spread through mosquito bites, but yellow 'cause he's afraid to meet Dick Tiger in the boxing ring! (*Emphatically*) I say Fullmer is yellow! I say he's yellow; he is not nursing a bruised ankle. He is talking a load of codswallop to mislead the public, (*Quickly*) but it is not working!

REPORTER, *finishing up scribbling notes about Diamond's comments*. The final date for the Tiger-Fullmer bout, as you stated, is August 10. That's the middle of the rainy season in Nigeria; what measures, if any, have been adopted to ensure that the event is not hampered by the incessant rains that occur here at this time of the year?

JACK SOLOMONS, *attempting to answer*. Well, uh, we—(*Chief Johnson walks in.*)

CHIEF JMJ, *surprised*. Well, what a pleasant surprise! Bobby, Jack, I see that you are enjoying your stay in our very hospitable country of Nigeria!

JACK SOLOMONS, *smiling*. Yes, good morning, Chief Johnson. (*They shake hands.*)

BOBBY DIAMOND, *shaking the chief's hand*. Good morning, Chief.

REPORTER, *quickly shifting his microphone to Chief Johnson*. Good morning, Chief Johnson.

CHIEF JMJ, *jokingly.* Ah, ah, what are you, Mr. Reporter, doing here when my friends are trying to have their breakfast peaceably?

REPORTER, *seeming apologetic.* Pardon me, sir. I just wanted to know what other plans are put in place should the rains prove menacing. The rains in Nigeria, as we know, can be quite torrential.

CHIEF JOHNSON. I want to assure ticket holders that there is absolutely no cause for alarm. The fight will go on as planned. *(Quickly changing the topic.)* Very positive news has been received from Fullmer and his manager, Marv Jensen. They regret very much the necessity of postponing the fight to August 10 due to Fullmer's foot injury. They have lately confirmed that they will be arriving into the country on the twentieth of July, so that Fullmer can continue his training here in our world-class gym. People should please go and purchase tickets for the bout. There are a lot of incentives for ticket holders, so please, Nigerians, patriotic Nigerians, go and purchase those tickets for our national honor and our prestige in the world's view.

REPORTER. Venerable Chief, what would be the incentive for purchasing tickets to the Tiger-Fullmer bout?

CHIEF JMJ, *clearing his throat.* Every public worker in the eastern and western regions who purchases tickets for the fight will be granted a two-day holiday in order to allow them to make travel arrangements to the bout. Ticket holders in the northern region will receive four days off to permit them to make arrangements et cetera. *(Pause)* In addition, the federal government has arranged with the various mass transportation systems for reduced fares for ticket holders coming to Liberty Stadium in Ibadan. Extra transport has been added to and from Ibadan. *(Pause)* The latest postponement will only allow

Nigerians more time to save up money to purchase tickets for the fight.

REPORTER, *elated*. That's encouraging, Your Excellency, but are there plans in place to ensure that the audience at the fight scene will be shielded from getting soaking wet in the open-air arena at Liberty Stadium?

CHIEF JMJ, *cheerfully*. Rest assured that we have everything under control! (*Pause*) People aren't buying tickets because they think the fight will be a washout, and as with some old habits that die hard, some members of the Nigerian public continue to adhere to beliefs in gods and demigods. Therefore, (*Clearing his throat.*) in order to appease that segment of the public, I have engaged the services of a rain doctor to ensure that the rain gods are placated in order to keep the rains at bay on the day of this historic bout. (*With both hands upraised, he speaks gleefully.*) Repair crews are toiling around the clock to patch up all highways leading up to Ibadan. As we speak, construction for over fifteen thousand bicycle stands is underway outside of the Liberty Stadium. (*Pause*) We have also gone the extra mile to ensure the safety of ticket buyers, as we envision a multitude of people descending on the scene of the fight. For the purpose of safety and orderliness, we have commissioned the services of veteran troops of the United Nations, along with police and army contingents, to help maintain law and order. (*Waving at the reporter, he speaks emphatically.*) Go! Tell the public that all roads lead to Liberty Stadium in Ibadan, come August 10, 1963!

REPORTER, *sweetly*. At your service, Chief Johnson. (*He exits.*)

JACK SOLOMONS, *in disbelief* Chief Johnson, do you really believe in the authenticity of the claims of these (*mumbles*) rain doctors?

CHIEF JMJ, *startled*. Huh? Oh, well, I don't personally believe in the efficacy of their craft, but quite a few members of society bank on their whims as their source of weather forecasting. (*Adjusting his agbada.*) At my wedding ceremony years ago, I contracted the services of a rain doctor just to pacify some of my guests who still held on to those old beliefs.

BOBBY DIAMOND, *doubtfully*. So, how did things turn out?

JACK SOLOMONS. Did it rain?

CHIEF JMJ, *throwing both hands in the air*. Oh, it rained cats and dogs!

(*They all laugh.*)

JACK SOLOMONS. How is it that people still patronize them?

CHIEF JMJ. You know that saying, "Old habits die hard"? (*He pauses, adjusts his glasses, and continues.*) I have only offered to give them half of the total amount they requested, anyway.

BOBBY DIAMOND, *shocked* Well, how many of these rain doctors did you hire, Chief?

JACK SOLOMONS, *concurring*. Yeah! How many, Chief?

CHIEF JMJ, *fidgeting with his glasses and cap*. Well, since I live in the capital city of Lagos, I hired one from Lagos. He came highly recommended. However, I'd need to hire another one from the host city of Ibadan in order to avoid any jealousies and conflicts that may arise between the rain doctors. I will pay them a thousand pounds, only half the amount agreed upon, to complete payment only when, or if they can deliver on their promise to keep the rains at bay for the event. (*Pause*) I had to employ this precautionary measure considering a national embarrassment brought about by their incompetence some years ago.

BOBBY DIAMOND, *probing*. Whi—

CHIEF JMJ, *interrupting*. That'll be for another time, Bobby. So, is the food here good?

(*They laugh.*)

SCENE TWO

DICK TIGER SR. I had been training intensely, so much that my manager, Jersey Jones, and trainer, Jimmy August, are worried that I might burn out from all the training and the postponements. Solomons, however, brought confirmation of Fullmer's arrival date and the date of the bout.

(*A sparring session at the Abalti Army Barracks*)

JIMMY AUGUST, *directing*. Retreat a little, Tiger, you are moving too close to your opponent! (*Tiger ignores him.*) You can wear yourself out quicker when you don't retreat as often as you jab! (*Realizing that Tiger is continuing to jab away at his sparring partner, he grabs and swiftly moves the sparrer away from Tiger's barrage of punches.*) Tiger! Tiger, what are you doing?

DICK TIGER, *startled*. What's that for, Jimmy?

JIMMY AUGUST. Dick, you are punching too hard without listening to instructions! You seem a little distracted? (*Pause.*) Besides, you don't want to kill your poor sparring partner.

DICK TIGER, *looking at the sparring partner apologetically*. I am sorry. Please pardon me.

Tiger sparring.

Trying to stay conditioned.

JIMMY AUGUST. Fullmer's indecisiveness is really getting to you. (*Pause*) If he thinks that he cannot face you in the ring, then he should come out and say so. There are a lot of guys waiting for a chance at the middleweight championship!

DICK TIGER, *untying his gloves.* Jersey should have been here in Nigeria by now also. He should have reached out to inform us of the latest developments regarding Fullmer's condition. (*Suddenly angry.*) We are both champions, so what could Fullmer be so afraid of?

JIMMY AUGUST. If I knew that—(*Solomons walks in with some papers.*)

JACK SOLOMONS, *cheerfully.* Hello, everyone! Dick Tiger, I hear that you've been training with the focus of a famished eagle, ready to swoop up some dinner! (*Laughing, he quickly turns serious upon noticing Tiger's distaste for the quip. He clears his throat.*) I wanted to confirm to you directly that Fullmer will be in Nigeria on the twentieth of July.

DICK TIGER. The fight is still on for the tenth as earlier confirmed?

JACK SOLOMONS. Yes. The fight is slated to be held on the tenth of August, unequivocally.

DICK TIGER. Have you heard anything from Jers— (*Jersey Jones walks into the gym.*)

JERSEY JONES. Here I am, Tiger. I had been trying to reach you guys, but the phone lines have not been cooperative, so I thought I'd fly in, especially since it's reported that Fullmer and his team will be arriving next week.

JACK SOLOMONS. I just heard from Jensen. He's confirmed their date of arrival, and we have scheduled the fight for the tenth of August.

JERSEY JONES. *adamant.* Look, they've dillydallied before, so we have to take whatever they say with a grain of salt, until we actually see them here in Nigeria! There are lots of guys lining up to have their chance at a world-championship title! If he continues to prevaricate, I'll not hesitate to draft Joey Giardello from Philadelphia, or the Hungarian boxer Laszlo Papps right away!

JACK SOLOMONS. It's official, Jersey. (*Showing the telegrammed message.*) They sent missives of their arrival plans through the American ambassador.

JERSEY JONES. If Fullmer does not show up for this fight, he can rest assured that he will never have another opportunity to vie for the world middleweight championship, ever!

S c e n e   T h r e e

DICK TIGER SR. Fullmer's camp finally arrived in Nigeria as planned. His entourage included his manager, Marv Jensen; his father, Lawrence "Tuff" Fullmer; and a sparring partner, Milo Savage. They were pleased to be in the country, and Jack Solomons was on hand to welcome them at the Ikeja Airport.

(*At the Ikeja Airport*)

JACK SOLOMONS. Hello, hello.

GENE FULLMER. Hello, Jack. (*Pointing to his escorts.*) Meet my father, Tuff, and of course you know Marv Jensen, my manager. This is Milo, my sparring partner.

JACK SOLOMONS, *shaking their hands.* Delighted to meet you.

GENE FULLMER. Some warm, breezy weather they have here.

MARV JENSEN. It's a beautiful country, nothing like I had imagined.

JACK SOLOMONS. The food is good here, too. C'mon, guys, I'll escort you to your hotel. When you're settled into your rooms, please meet us this evening in the ballroom of the hotel for a dinner reception in honor of the two boxing titans!

GENE FULLMER. Very gracious of you. Will do.

MARV JENSEN. See you later. Thanks.

SCENE FOUR

DICK TIGER SR. Fullmer and his entourage joined their hosts, Hogan Bassey and Jack Solomons, with one hundred fifty other guests in the hotel's ballroom. To their amazement, they were warmly received by the Nigerian populace, but not before strained relations between Marv Jensen and Bobby Diamond erupted in a verbal spat at the dinner reception. Exchanges tapered off on a cheery, positive note however, thanks to the interjection of some comic relief by the ebullient Chief Johnson.

(*In the ballroom at the Federal Palace Hotel*)

HOGAN BASSEY. Venerable ladies and gentlemen, you are cordially welcomed to this auspicious meet in honor of two very special and accomplished world-champion boxers, in the persons of Nigeria's Dick Tiger and America's Gene Fullmer. (*Applause*) We want to officially welcome them and wish them a healthful and rewarding outing in our country.

JACK SOLOMONS, *taking the microphone from Bassey.* Ladies and Gentlemen, champions, you are welcome to this gathering, a prelude to an epochal event in boxing's history—in Nigeria's history. The whole world will be watching, in less than a month, a duel of epic proportions between Gene Fullmer and Dick Tiger. (*Audience applauds*) It is a fight like none other in the history of Africa and the world! Ladies and gentlemen, I present to you the two boxing titans who will help make this boxing history come to pass. I present to you the middleweight boxing champion of the world, Dick Tiger of Nigeria (*Thunderous applause.*) and his challenger for the crown, Gene Fullmer, the former middleweight boxing king. (*They applaud. The combatants acknowledge the crowd by standing and taking a bow.*)

HOGAN BASSEY. Here! Here! Now, let's eat. Bon appétit!

DICK TIGER, *walking up to Fullmer and Jensen.* Hello, guys. For a moment there, I thought there was not going to be a Tiger-Fullmer bout in Nigeria. (*Looking at Fullmer.*) Are you okay now?

GENE FULLMER. Hey, Tiger. (*Guiltily*) I am sorry about that. I apologize to the whole country, but nothing about the postponements was done intentionally.

DICK TIGER. So, you are ready to give my people a good fight? I know that they've forgiven you already. We are very forgiving people. (*Demonstrating*) They are just glad that they are now able to see their illustrious son display his world-renowned boxing skills before them.

(*They laugh.*)

GENE FULLMER. Okay, Tiger. We'll give them a good fight! (*Pause*) And may the best fighter win.

BOBBY DIAMOND, *overhearing the conversation.* Please, we do not want any more bloody cat-and-mouse games. People have held on to their tickets for too long to be bamboozled any longer.

MARV JENSEN, *exploding at Bobby*. How dare you, Bobby Diamond, try to throw slime Gene's way! You are unconscionable! You are sickening! (*To his listeners.*) At first, he alleges to reporters that Fullmer is yellow; now (*Scowling*) he has the gall to insinuate that there's a game of cat-and-mouse going on? Disgusting! (*Quickly.*) You owe Gene an apology!

BOBBY DIAMOND, *yelling*. Fullmer is culpable, and you owe the apology, Jensen, for playing along in this deceptive game! (*Gesturing*) I have had my admiration for Fullmer, but on this occasion, I say he is yellow and still think so!

MARV JENSEN, *retorting*. Gene Fullmer is one of the greatest middleweights to ever walk the face of the earth! So, your words mean nothing!

BOBBY DIAMOND. Marv Jensen, if you think that Fullmer is great, I think Tiger is greater, and Fullmer will fall at the feet of the Tiger! I have watched Tiger box a three-round session with spar mate, Bob Zico. (*Emphatically*) Tiger will knock Fullmer out!

MARV JENSEN, *livid*. Please! Fullmer is in good shape and will have no weight difficulty. He'll be at his peak just before the fight!

JACK SOLOMONS, *interrupting*. Guys, gentlemen, stop this! It does not look good at all in front of our guests of honor. Please, gentlemen, sheathe your swords.

CHIEF JMJ, *animated*. You know what? We'll add Marv and Bobby as part of the preliminaries in the fight. Yeah! The Jenson versus Diamond fight! (*Listeners laugh.*) Or (*Pause*) better still, I'm going to take both of them on myself! (*Gesturing*) Let's go! (*Spectators are bowled over, laughing.*)

JACK SOLOMONS, *to the guests.* You can always count on the good chief to save the day. (*Pause*) Now, please, let us enjoy our dinner!

GENE FULLMER, *aside to Jensen.* Marv, you didn't have to dignify Bobby Diamond's comments with a response. Your responses seem to have added validity to his madness.

MARV JENSEN. It does seem that way. I'm sorry, I couldn't bear to watch him slander your good name with such impunity, and knowing within me that you are an honorable man (*pauses*) none of this was your fault. But they don't know—

GENE FULLMER, *interrupting.* Relax, Marv! Forget about it. It's all behind us now! Please, let's focus on the upcoming fight, to give the people of Nigeria a fight for the ages!

MARV JENSEN. Here! Here! Let's do that.

Scene Five

DICK TIGER SR. At the reception, Bobby Diamond, in an attempt to calm his frayed nerves following his feud with Jensen, consumed a little too much of the wine and whiskey served and; he became inebriated. As a result of the drunkenness he was incapacitated and was unable to make it solo to his hotel room after the reception. Solomons and Hogan Bassey graciously took on the task of helping Bobby to his room. They dropped him off and left. Bobby crashed into his bed with a loud thud, and was lulled into deep sleep by alcohol. Moments later though, he bolted up from his bed, confused.

(*At the hotel, Solomons and Bassey are helping Diamond up to his room.*)

JACK SOLOMONS, *breathing rapidly from the lifting.* I can't believe this bloke emptied a bloody bottle of whisky all by himself. Look at his eyes! (*Diamond, barely able to keep his eyes open, lets out a big burp.*)

BOBBY DIAMOND, *half groggy.* Paa'don.

HOGAN BASSEY, *wincing.* Hey, easy!

JACK SOLOMONS, *peering at Diamond's eyes, jokingly.* Look at your eyes! They're as red as that bottle of wine you chugged!

HOGAN BASSEY, *teasing.* Mmmm, they do look very red (*mumbling*) Oh, wait, they're (*mumbles*) yellow?

JACK SOLOMONS. Maybe, maybe he's got (*pauses*) yellow fever?

HOGAN BASSEY, *laughing softly.* Then we'd better get out of here, quick!

JACK SOLOMONS. Yeah! (*They let him in his room and head back out the door.*)

(*Hours later, alone in his hotel room*)

BOBBY DIAMOND, *eyes almost shooting out of their sockets.* Grrrrh! Oh, I'm burning up! (*Rubbing and feeling all over his body, he begins to shiver violently, bewildered and frightened.*) Crickey Moses! Gor blimey! I've got (*mumbles*) fever! (*Still in bed, screaming and shaking uncontrollably.*) Gor blimey! (*Shocked*) I've got malaria fever? (*Pauses*) Yellow fever! (*Shrieking, he leaps from his bed, stumbling to the mirror.*) I've got yellow fever? I've bloody go' yellow fever? (*Pauses*) Crickey Moses! (*He peers at himself in the mirror and is relieved.*) Oh! (*Pauses*) Thank God! (*Pauses*) I'm jus' drunk! (*Moaning, eyes now half shut*) I'm just bloody drank (*mumbling*) dass all! (*Smiling faintly, eyes drooping, he stumbles hurriedly to the bathroom, empties his bladder, and trudges back to the room.*) I ain' go' no bloody yellow fever. I jus' drunk. (Like a sack of potatoes *he crashes back into bed, snoring.*)

SCENE SIX

DICK TIGER SR. Fullmer's presence in Nigeria and his resolve to duel with their favored son, me, quickly endeared him to the hearts of the Nigerian people. Huge crowds followed Fullmer's every move. Hundreds converged daily at the University of Ibadan Gymnasium, paying a one-shilling (fourteen cents) entrance fee to watch his workouts in readiness for the fight. Like the New York Stock Exchange, dwindling ticket sales were now on the rise with the news of Fullmer's arrival in the country. The people of Nigeria were now gripped with "fight fever."

(*Taking a break from workouts at the gymnasium*)

GENE FULLMER. I cannot believe the level of camaraderie and acceptance that's being accorded us in this journey.

MARV JENSEN. These people are extremely gracious, especially after the postponements and seeming animosity that threatened to abort the highly anticipated fight, one would think that they'd hate us.

(*Tuff and Milo enter.*)

GENE FULLMER, *to Tuff and Milo.* Would you believe that about 150,000 people lined the main streets of Ibadan to serenade us by singing my name on our way to the Oba's Palace, for a welcome reception chanting, "Fullmer!

Fullmer!"

(*They laugh.*)

MARV JENSEN. They follow us to the sparring sessions, each one of them willing to pay a shilling, which is a sizeable amount here, just to watch Gene train for the fight.

(*Enter Jack Solomons.*)

GENE FULLMER. I'm very delighted by the turn of events here. Things could have really taken a turn for the worse, but the reverse is the case. Hey, I think some of them might even root for me at the fight!

JACK SOLOMONS, *sarcastically*. Oh yeah, a handful, maybe. It looks like even the crocodiles are on Dick Tiger's side for this fight.

JENSEN, FULLMER, TUFF, and MILO, *in unison*. Huh?

MARV JENSEN, What d'ya mean, crocodiles?

JACK SOLOMONS, *mysteriously*. Well, this one could be folklore, written in modern-day Nigeria. Word has it that in a town called Oje, not far from the Liberty Stadium, lives a revered crocodile, which the locals believe possesses the powers to grant all good things when sacrifices of live chickens are made to it. They throw chickens into the river to appease it (*Pause*) uh ... him (or) uh ... her when they need a favor. (*Pause*) They believe that Tiger will win because they—

HOGAN BASSEY, *overhearing the statement as he's walking in*. Hi, guys. (*Jokingly*) Well, you forgot to mention that there are hardly any more chickens left in Oje from all the chickens they've been throwing in the pool lately. (*Grinning*) My goodness! People should just relax. Dick Tiger was able to win the first two championships without that sort of sacrifice and depletion of a very vital source of protein! (*They laugh.*) Yes, there are hardly any more chickens for those people to supplement their diets. (*Quickly*) Oh, and have you heard about the rain doctors? (*To Solomons*) Did you tell them about the rain doctors Chief Johnson hired?

JACK SOLOMONS. Oh, but he's hired another one, from Ibadan … in order not to stir any jealousies or animosities between rain doctors in Lagos and the host city of Ibadan. (*He throws his hands up.*) Go figure!

HOGAN BASSEY. According to published reports, the Ibadan rainmakers grew jealous when they learned that the rainmakers from Lagos are getting paid such huge sums. So, in order to get their piece of the national cake, courtesy of Chief JMJ, they trumped up the charge that the Lagos rain doctors have no jurisdiction to "practice" in Ibadan, and they are threatening to thwart the efforts of the Lagos rain doctors, hence the chief's intervention.

JACK SOLOMONS, *laughing.* This is like a bloody franchise. It's a scam! (*mumbles*) Oh, you will be the death of me yet. (*Pauses*) Methinks they're all just a bunch o' snake oil salesmen, bloody laughing all the way to the bank—at their people's expense!

HOGAN BASSEY, *embarrassed, hastily nods in agreement.* Ignorance can be expensive. (*He laughs nervously.*) But it's said that he is paying them only half of the agreed sum of a thousand pounds with the agreement that if there's rain during the fight, they don't get the balance of the money.

MARV JENSEN, *skeptical.* You're kidding!

(*They laugh uncontrollably.*)

HOGAN BASSEY, *suddenly getting serious.* No! Well, uh, I know that it's stories like these that cause you guys in the Western world to assume that we are cannibals or barbaric, eh?

GENE FULLMER, *with a smirk.* Don't look at me—ask Dick Tiger, he's the one who goes around saying, (*Animatedly*) "We eat humoan beings, medium rare, for breakfast." (*They laugh hysterically.*)

HOGAN BASSEY. I can imagine the kind of ridiculous questions posed to him by reporters that must've necessitated such a sarcastic response.

GENE FULLMER, *in disbelief.* Some of the reporters, to my chagrin, have the gall to ask Dick whether Africans live in trees. Those kinds of prompts vicariously bias the minds of people; the majority of whom have not been to Africa.

MARV JENSEN: But we've been enlightened by what we've witnessed here in Nigeria. The people have been nothing but gracious and civil toward us. They are very religious too! Why, I didn't know that there are about sixty thousand Nigerians who are already practicing the Mormon faith, even without the priesthood to bless the sacrament. Many more have expressed a desire to join in our Mormon faith and doctrines. They ask about appropriate songs to sing, so I promised to get them the Latter-Day Saints hymnals. (*Exhilarated*) It's been amazing. This is one of the most rewarding experiences of my life!

GENE FULLMER, *agreeing.* It really has been a very enlightening experience.

HOGAN BASSEY. Do, please, help to spread the good news, folks, when you return to America—Africans are not barbaric or cannibalistic!

JACK SOLOMONS, *jokingly*. Hogan, I'm sure you didn't come all the way here just to give a bloody lecture about the West's treatment of Africa.

HOGAN BASSEY, *cheerfully*. It's all in the mix, Jack! However, I did want to share the good news that ticket sales have skyrocketed since Gene's arrival to Nigeria!

JACK SOLOMONS. Oh, yeah. The other day, the governor-general, Dr. Azikiwe, called a press conference where he urged Nigerians to go out and purchase tickets for the fight, and on the spot, he purchased ten ringside tickets for himself and some members of his cabinet!

HOGAN BASSEY. The deputy premier of the western region, Chief Obafemi Awolowo, also purchased tickets for his cabinet members, while in the north, the government has granted a four-day-long break for its employees who purchase tickets for the fight.

JACK SOLOMONS, *dutifully*. This fight is going to go down in history as one of the greatest (*Pause*) if not the greatest showcase in prizefight history. The Nigerian government has gone out of its way to ensure that this showcase is overwhelmingly a success!

HOGAN BASSEY, *excited*. Even the Nigerian Army is cooperating by deploying two hundred fifty of their men to serve as ushers for the event! Fifteen hundred police are scheduled to patrol the eighty-nine miles of highway between Lagos and Ibadan. And don't forget that Chief Johnson is stirring a lot of interest of his own (*Pauses)* He is ordering (*emphatically*) the Nigerian Boxing Board of Control (NBBC) to issue him a permit so that he can challenge Jack Toller, a retired Ghanaian heavyweight boxer in a preliminary bout at the Tiger-Fullmer Fight!

JACK SOLOMONS, *obliviously*. Did they issue him the permit?

HOGAN BASSEY. No way! (*Laughing*) He threatened to disband them, but it's all in jest, all in the spirit of publicity for the upcoming fight. (*Pause*) Actually, the prime minister himself, Alhaji Sir Abubakar Tafawa Balewa, got in the spirit too. He said to Chief Johnson, "Joseph J., I do not care if you box or not, but make sure you insure yourself sufficiently." (*They laugh*).

JACK SOLOMONS, *laughing*. Hogan, let's get back to work! We've got to ensure that everything goes according to plan for the big fight.

HOGAN BASSEY. Yeah. (*Halting*) Hey, anyone heard from Bobby since the other night?

JACK SOLOMONS, *laughing*. Oh, poor Bobby. (*Mumbling*) He's alright. Told me he had a rough night and serious hangover, but 'll meet up with us before evening.

JACK SOLOMONS and HOGAN BASSEY, *snickering*.

HOGAN BASSEY. Yeah, (*laughing*) too much alcohol would do that to you.

JACK SOLOMONS and HOGAN BASSEY, *leaving*. See you later, guys.

JACK SOLOMONS. Good luck with the training, Gene.

GENE FULLMER. Thanks, guys. Nice to see you!

Scene Seven

DICK TIGER SR. I took time off from my regimented training sessions to call my darling wife, Abigail to inquire about how she and the children were coping. My conscience compelled me to apologize for my inability to call as frequently as I would prefer because of my hectic workout schedule for the upcoming bout.

DICK TIGER, *on the phone*. Hello, my dear wife.

ABIGAIL. Oh, ezigbo di'm, (my precious husband) how are you doing today?

DICK TIGER. I'm well, thank you. Please forgive me for not calling in a while. My training is taking up most of my time.

ABIGAIL. I know that. I also know that it is important to you and the rest of Nigeria. (*Pause*) It's amazing how this fight has brought people together. Don't worry, just stay focused and calm.

TIGER, *lovingly*. Yes, my dear. I can always count on your wisdom and understanding. (*Pause*) How are my children?

ABIGAIL. They are asleep now, but we are all fine. Really, we just want you to stay healthy and stay focused. We know the significance of the upcoming fight. (*Perking up*.) You know, your townsmen have appointed two delegates to represent them at the fight. They are your young secretary, Mr. Ebere Ihejirika, and Nze Timothy B. Osuala.

DICK TIGER. Oh, that's nice. I'll try and meet with them after the fight. We hope all goes well. (*Pause*) Fullmer is a very tough man, so if I want to win by a knockout, I must train harder than ever!

Abigail, *admiringly*. That's my husband! The Lord is your strength. May He keep you.

DICK TIGER. I love you. Give my love, too, to my kids.

ABIGAIL. I'll do that. Take good care of yourself. Bye.

Abigail in native garb. Circa, 1984.

Act Eleven

(It is now late afternoon, and the friends are still very alert, brimming with excitement, and a sense of euphoria at the stories of Tiger's exploits and the mind-boggling negotiations that led up to the big fight in Ibadan.)

DICK TIGER SR, *rubbing his hands.* It's now time to go into— the blast heard throughout the world, from Liberty Stadium in the ancient city of Ibadan!

GODWIN. Eyiooh! It is you third and last fight with Fulluma!

CHORUS, *excitedly.* Fulluma! Tiga! Fulluma! Tiga!

GOLDSMITH. The number one big fight to take place in Africa!

DICK TIGER SR. Correct! Correct! Correct! Now, if you think that some of the events so far have been fantastic, well, fasten your seatbelts for some more head-spinning scenarios leading up to the big fight!

GOLDSMITH, *eyes glistening with excitement.* Let's go!

Dick Tiger Sr. Final preparations for the fight ensued. The entire country of Nigeria was abuzz with anticipation of the Tiger-Fullmer bout; even warring politicians called a truce just for the fight. Foreign press corps and international radio and satellite stations were setting up shop in Ibadan for the transmittal of the fight. Prominent chiefs from neighboring West African countries, such as Ghana, Sierra Leone, Togo, and Gambia, arrived in Ibadan by airplane and boat. The eyes of the world, it seemed, have turned on Nigeria!

(*Near the construction site at Liberty Stadium*)

CHIEF JMJ, *to a member of the press corps*. Work here in the stadium is near completion. (*Pointing*) Due to the heavy downpour the past couple of days, we have repair crews working 'round the clock to patch up all roads leading up to the Liberty Stadium that have been weathered by the rainy season's cloudbursts.

FOREIGN REPORTER, *suspiciously*. Your Excellency, we hear that all the hotels in both Lagos and Ibadan are booked to capacity with people coming to see the historic fight. Could you share some of the measures your team has put in place to manage the multitude of people that will descend on the Liberty Stadium for this showcase?

CHIEF JMJ, *adjusting his spectacles*. A battalion of soldiers and police have been contracted by the government to prevent and quell any uprisings that might occur at or near the stadium. We have also deployed about two hundred police to patrol the city and direct traffic. (*Bragging*) We are not taking any chances with this event; we want to demonstrate to the world through the successful hosting of this epic fight, that Nigeria, though a fledgling nation with barely three years of independence, can hold its own among other civilized and independent nations. (*Pause*) Actually, in the same week that we are hosting this great fight, Nigeria will make a bid on the international scene to have Lagos, the capital of Nigeria, named the headquarters for the newly formed Organization of African Unity (OAU)!

FOREIGN REPORTER. That's fantastic!

(*Bobby Diamond walks in.*)

CHIEF JMJ, *proudly*. Oh Yes! We are the giant of Africa!

BOBBY DIAMOND. Hello, Chief Johnson. I see work at the site is in full swing!

CHIEF JMJ. Hello, Bobby, we're almost set for D-day! (*Ecstatic*) You can't hold the floodwaters back! (*He spreads his hands wide open.*) The gates are wide open!

FOREIGN REPORTER, *probing*. But, Chief Johnson, if you don't mind me asking, with the temperature levels well into the nineties, how are you going to control the heat in the stadium with thousands of people expected to converge in the open-air arena?

CHIEF JMJ, *slightly amused*. Huh? Have you been in Madison Square Garden on a fight-night? (*Animatedly*) It's a giant sauna! Crowded, humid, and smoke-filled from the cigar-chomping patrons! (*Adjusting his agbada.*) Besides, most of the time, people aren't paying attention to anything but the fight! The focus is usually entirely on the boxers (*pauses*) It's all about the fight. Nothing else matters!

FOREIGN REPORTER. Well, thank you very much for your time, Chief Johnson.

CHIEF JMJ. That's all right. We hope that you enjoy the fight.

(*Exit reporter.*)

BOBBY DIAMOND, *incredulously.* More reporters and TV crews are arriving daily. The traffic bureau chief, Leonard Sealey, has arranged to bridge the Ibadan-London radio signal to the London–New York cable, stretching about an eight-thousand-mile line of direct communication to carry brief round-by-round descriptions of the fight from New York to Salt Lake City, Utah.

CHIEF JMJ. Oh, but that's not all. Kenneth Whitings and Denny Neeld, the ringside team who will help to transmit the event, will report from ringside eighty miles to a ship docked in Lagos Harbor via radio to the Syncom satellite, which will relay it to Fort Monmouth, New Jersey. From there, it will be telegraphed into New York sports stations via Western Union. It is a very intricate setup to ensure complete closed-circuit coverage of the event.

BOBBY DIAMOND. Things are gradually but surely falling into place for the showcase. I'm just coming from Tiger's training site, and they are working very hard to get the Tiger in top condition for the fight. (*Pause*) I also stopped by Fullmer's camp. Training is also in full swing; however, (*His countenance changes.*) Jensen is calling for a press conference to—

CHIEF JMJ, *puzzled.* For what?

BOBBY DIAMOND. He's talking up a load of codswallop again. (*Deliberately slowing his speech.*) Jensen is unhappy about Solomon's choice of a British referee ... for the event.

CHIEF JMJ. But what does it matter? Jack Hart is a world-renowned professional boxing referee. We cannot do much about that now; we have only a couple more days to the fight.

BOBBY DIAMOND, *exhaustedly*. He's insinuating that there may be some hanky-panky going on between Solomons, Jack, and me being that the three of us are British. (*Astonished.*) Can you believe it? He's blinkered! (Crazy!)

CHIEF JMJ, *perplexed*. That's absurd!

BOBBY DIAMOND. But that's what he believes!

CHIEF JMJ. Leave it to me. I'll talk to him.

BOBBY DIAMOND. Okay, Chief. I'll see you later. (*He leaves.*)

CHIEF JMJ, *shaking his head in disbelief.* Bye.

Scene Two

DICK TIGER SR. Only four days to the Tiger-Fullmer showdown, Fullmer's manager, Marv Jensen, was expressing discontent over the promoter's choice of Jack Hart as the referee for the event. He called a news conference to air his grievances about the manner of protocols. In attendance were Marv Jensen, Gene Fullmer, Jack Solomons, and some members of the national and international press.

(*The press corps gathers at the site of Fullmer's training camp.*)

MARV JENSEN, *stoically*. Ladies and Gentlemen, welcome to today's briefing. Certain extenuating developments that may compromise the outcome of this most anticipated and epochal fight have necessitated my desire for this meeting with you, the members of the press. (*Pause*) Now, there are two principal players in this event—Dick Tiger of Nigeria and Gene Fullmer of West Jordan, USA. (*He places his hands in his pockets.*) Lately, a crucial decision was made about a suitable referee for the event. A referee was chosen but without my consultation or input. I, therefore, suspect foul play on the part of the promoter, Jack Solomons, who is British. Bobby Diamond, Tiger's manager, is also British, as is Jack Hart, who has been contracted to referee the upcoming bout.

REPORTER, *confused*. Mr. Jensen, are you suggesting that due to the fact that the promoter, referee, and the manager are of the same nationality, your client, Gene Fullmer, might not get a fair call at the fight?

MARV JENSEN. I have issues basically with the manner with which I was overlooked in the selection process for a referee. (*Shrieking*) This referee would be overseeing a major event where my client is one of the principal players, and I just wanted to share my distaste of the whole scenario with the general public!

The boxing gloves come on!

JACK SOLOMONS, *impatiently*. Mr. Jensen, Jersey Jones, and Bobby Diamond, Tiger's handlers, were very much aware of the nomination of Jack Hart as referee for the event.

MARV JENSEN, *growing angry*. Why was I not informed of this fact until now? I think that it is well within my rights to be privy to such information!

JACK SOLOMONS, *livid*. Well, Mr. Jensen, I fail to see how it is your place to be party to the bloody decision-making process here! (*Pause*) The Nigerian Boxing Board of Control (NBBC) put in a request to the British Boxing Board of Control and got Mr. Jack Hart. Who are you to object, Jensen, when Aibis Akerele, secretary to the Nigerian Boxing Commission wrote to the British Board of Control, asking for the nomination of a reputable referee? (*Gesturing*) He asked, and they got a reputable referee, in the person of Mr. Jack Hart! (*Speaking slowly and deliberately.*) He will be refereeing the highly anticipated Tiger-Fullmer bout, slated to happen this Saturday, August 10, 1963. (*Suddenly speaking quickly and audaciously.*) Ladies and gentlemen, if you haven't purchased your tickets for the fight, please do so as soon as possible! All roads lead to Liberty Stadium come August 10!

MARV JENSEN, *boldly*. Thank you for your audience, ladies and gentlemen of the press. We will see you at the fight! (*They disperse.*)

Scene Three

GOLDSMITH. The rain did an encore prior to dissipating with the clouds. It pounded and pelted raindrops all over the city of Ibadan, completely halting traffic and imposing a lockdown on all activities. Conversely, as promised by Chief JMJ, two rain doctors, Sangogbemi and Sangodiran, appeared at a crossroads in the vicinity of Liberty Stadium, in a session to appease Sango, their rain god. The rain doctors were scantily clad in white cloth tied around their waists, their faces and chests covered in tribal markings. Each of them clutched a white feather in one hand and an old clay pot in the other. They both laid the pots on the ground, and glared intently at each other, as if channeling a medium. Then, rigidly, they stormed off in opposite directions. Looking upward, they raised their white feathers and the pots toward the sky and proceeded to chant and make invocations. They pled with Sango to "withhold the rains from falling on the city of Ibadan." As if provoked by their presence, rain, thunder, and lightning form a concerto, putting on a command performance! Rain beat hard on the tin roofs, with thunder and lightning providing backup. Suddenly, the wind joined in, breathing boisterously, whirling tin cans and debris there and about, all over the freshly tarred roads of Ibadan in a crescendo of sounds! Rain doctors energized their chants, and with that, lightening zigzagged intermittently across the crying sky, as if in a waltz. The rain doctors, Sangogbemi and Sangodiran, continued their deluge of chanting and pleas, and the rains seemed to be stealing away. The rain, regaining momentum, rapturously whipped the bronze and ebony-skinned natives wading through muddied puddles of water, oblivious to the ensuing power struggle. With their garb clinging to their bodies, as if in fear. The rain doctors intensified their chants, and consequently, the rain seemed to be fizzling away as quickly as it came. The moaning of the wind began to soften, and caressed the city, blowing specks of rain gently about until at last, the rains ceased!

SCENE FOUR

DICK TIGER SR. The weighing-in ceremony commenced on the morning of the fight amidst nearly clear skies and light showers. Getting to the Obisesan Auditorium, site of the weighing-in ceremony, proved an uphill battle for Fullmer and I as we were besieged by thousands of fans enroute to the venue, but I devised a plan to distract the pesky fans.

DICK TIGER, *with Bassey, pulling up a distance away from the rear of the Obisesan Auditorium.* Let's park here, away from the crowd. *(Pause)* They might delay our entry into the auditorium if they notice us.

With Mr. Slater (Left), Dr. Azikiwe, Chief Johnson and Hogan Bassey (Far right).

HOGAN BASSEY, *nodding in agreement)* That's a good idea.

(Tiger parks his recently delivered, top-of-the-line Mercedes Benz automobile blocks away from the venue.)

DICK TIGER. Let's enter quietly through the back entrance; that way, no one will detect us. *(They hear chanting,* "Full-mar! Full-mar! Full-mar!"*)* Oh, poor Fullmer *(Smirking)*, they've spotted him.

HOGAN BASSEY. Hope the policemen at the main entrance can help him ease his way inside, or he might be late for the weighing-in.

SCENE FIVE

DICK TIGER SR. In keeping with the requirements of weighing-in procedures, the two combatants, Fullmer and I, arrived dressed in our boxing shorts, with our managers and trainers in tow. Chief Johnson also showed up in his shorts as a potential participant. Solomons, Bassey, Diamond, and hundreds of other supporters and fight fans were present to witness the event. During the ceremony, supporters caused such an uproar that the stage of the local theater began to shake as they stamped their feet enthusiastically, chanting, "Tiga! Tiga! Tiga!" Their antics rendered the proceedings inaudible. Gene Fullmer and I stood, awaiting a weigh-in, when there came a quick smatter of giggles. The crowd had sighted Chief Johnson dressed in shorts, injecting himself between Gene and I, in a boxing stance. It took Diamond's and Solomons's intervention to restore order. With order restored the proceedings commenced with the boxing physicians checking our breathing and weight. Right after the ceremony, I stealthily made my way out of the building, through the rear egress. Fullmer, on the other hand, was mobbed by fans as he ventured through the front exit. The police had to intervene to wrestle him away from the doting crowd.

(*Inside the auditorium*)

CHIEF JMJ, *dramatically*. Ladies and gentlemen! You are welcome to the weigh-in ceremony! We are very elated that we have come to the tail end of preparations for this great contest between America's (*Pointing to Fullmer*) Gene Fullmer (*cheering*) and our own Di— (*They chant, "Tiga! Tiga!" and stamp their feet, this time rendering proceedings inaudible. Tiger and Fullmer mechanically take turns climbing on the official scale.*)

JACK SOLOMONS, *agitated, furtively asks for calm*. Ladies and Gentlemen, please (*mumbles*) we have to hear the results from the officers of this proceeding! (*The stomping and chanting continue, causing the stage of the theater to shake and the scales to jiggle.*) The officials are finding it bloody difficult to read the scales, due to the commotion!

BOBBY DIAMOND. Don't worry, we have the results. (*Vigorously ringing a handheld bell, he's able to get the attention of the audience. Clearing his throat, he makes the announcement.*) Fullmer weighed 160 pounds! (The crowd *cheers.*) And Dick Tiger scaled 159 ¾ pounds! (The crowd continues to *cheer and stomp,. Ignoring the outbursts, he continues.*) Thank you, ladies and gentlemen, for your presence at this auspicious weighing-in ceremony. (*Exhausted*) We will see you at the fight shortly! (*The hysterics are now deafening. Policemen, armed with batons, descend on the scene, and the crowd begins to disperse.*)

JERSEY JONES, *talking into Tiger's ear.* Meet us at the gym, ASAP.

DICK TIGER. All right. Bet you I'll get there before you. (*Jersey, unable to hear him, motions, but Tiger waves at him and stealthily exits the scene through the back entrance with Bassey in tow.*)

GENE FULLMER, *walking with Jensen toward Bobby and Solomons, anxiously.* Guys, you gotta help us outta here, quick. (*Desperately*) We've got preparations to conclude before the big show tonight!

MARV JENSEN. Yeah, it took us a good thirty minutes just to enter the building for the ceremony.

JACK SOLOMONS. Not to worry, we will ask the police to disperse the crowds, ASAP. (*Peering out the window.*) When you are able to get out of the building, hitch a ride with one of the reporters if you are unable to get to your car. (*Gasping*)

Don't know how easily you can penetrate the human blockade out there!

GENE FULLMER. We'll do. Thanks, guys.

MARV JENSEN, *gratefully*. Thank you.

JACK SOLOMONS. You're very welcome. See you tonight!

Scene Six

DICK TIGER SR. The entire nation of Nigeria was in a frenzy over the highly anticipated Tiger-versus-Fullmer fight. It had been raining for almost twenty-four hours, but, as if by heavenly command, the rains ceased and sunlight broke through, dissipating the clouds. Scores of people from all over the country converged on Ibadan by bus, truck, and plane. No-Vacancy signs were mounted on every hotel in the city, necessitating the erection of makeshift tents in designated locations around the Liberty Stadium. Solomons, thinking that there may not be enough seats, hastily arranged for a delivery of ten truckloads of chairs from ninety miles away.

(*At Liberty Stadium, Solomons and Bassey are finalizing preparations for the fight.*)

JACK SOLOMONS, *after surveying the prefight scene at Liberty Stadium*. I think we'd need to bring in a few thousand more chairs, to contain the anticipated number of people coming to the fight.

HOGAN BASSEY. It looks like that, but where are we going to get that many chairs now? The nearest ultramodern school is ninety miles away in Lagos.

JACK SOLOMONS. That's fine. Let's contact the trucking company of a friend of mine in Lagos and order the chairs for delivery to the stadium. They'd also be charged with promptly returning the chairs to the school after the big show.

HOGAN BASSEY. All right, let's do that, and hope it gets here well before showtime.

JACK SOLOMONS. I'll instruct the uniformed men to set them up inside the stadium as soon as they get here. (*They both leave hastily.*)

Act Twelve

SCENE ONE

GOLDSMITH. Crowds started to form four hours before the fight. A crowd of about thirty thousand people who could not afford the cheapest tickets stood by the gate of the Liberty Stadium, cheering the twenty-five thousand going in. The $1.50 seats—in the standing-room section, designed to contain six thousand—were sold out three hours before the fight. The $15.00 ringside section was full mostly because of the offer of free tickets to the soldiers and policemen. At dusk, the dignitaries and foreign diplomats began to arrive, filling up the $30.00 ringside seats. They included federal and regional ministers, regional premiers, boxing promoters, newsmen, and expatriate businessmen. There were also members of the parliament, members of the House of Chiefs, members of the Senate, and members of regional houses of assembly, as well as judges from federal and customary courts.

DICK TIGER SR. The announcer gave the audience an update on Chief JMJ's scheduled fight with the Ghanaian boxer. As the moment for the big fight came, amidst a fanfare of trumpets that reverberated in the stadium, the lights dim momentarily and returned to expose Gene Fullmer entering the ring, wearing red trunks and bouncing on his heels. The crowd roared approval.

Another momentary blackout occurred, and when the lights bounced back, yours truly, wearing blue boxing shorts and a silver robe joined Fullmer in the ring. This time, the crowd convulsed with excitement. After a rendition of the national anthems, Referee Jack Hart, clad in all-white trousers and a long-sleeve shirt, entered the ring with the announcer, who was clad in white blazer and solid black trousers. The announcer gave the audience an update on Chief JMJ's scheduled fight with the Ghanaian boxer. Jack Hart delivered the traditional prefight instructions, but his instructions fell on deaf ears as the audience was captivated by the two champion fighters on stage.

ANNOUNCER, *upon seeing Chief JMJ in the audience.* Uh *(Pause)* The Father of the Fight, Chief JMJ, was scheduled to box a heavyweight champion boxer from Ghana. (*The crowd snickers.*) But that fighter has chickened out; therefore, the chief, "The Father of the Fight," is declared the winner! (*The audience applauds, and there's also a smattering of laughter.*)

(*As trumpets sound, the lights go out and return to reveal Gene Fullmer.*)

ANNOUNCER. On my left, from America, is challenger, Gene Fullmer! (*Cheers. The lights are dimmed again and return, this time illuminating Dick Tiger.*) On my right, from Nigeria, is the reigning middleweight champion, Dick Tiger. (*The crowd's reaction is intense.*) At weigh-in this morning, Gene Fullmer weighed 160 pounds and Dick Tiger weighed 159 ¾ pounds. (*Pause*) Referee Jack Hart, recognized by the World Boxing Board of Control, is the referee for this fight tonight. Using the one-point system, the referee will be the sole judge in this showdown—unlike in America, where it is the referee and two judges. (*Pause*) Dick Tiger—champion, Gene Fullmer—challenger. (*Bell rings*) Round one!

ABIGAIL. My husband, though cautioned by his trainers not to be too anxious, especially in the opening rounds, threw caution to the wind and went on the prowl after Fullmer. He pinned Fullmer to the ropes several times in the first round with Fullmer sustaining a red welt on his face by the end of the round. The second round was more of the same, with Tiger throwing a barrage of left and right hooks to Fullmer's face and body. Before round two was over, Fullmer had a bruise over his left eye.

GOLDSMITH. Elated at the progression of the fight, Chief J.M. Johnson (Minister of Youth and Sports), T.O.S. Benson (Minister of Information), and Dr. K.O. Mbadiwe (Minister of State), popularly known by their nicknames derived from their initials, move around the ringside between rounds amid shouts of "JMJ!" "TOS!" and "KO!"

ANNOUNCER. This promises to be a very interesting fight. Fullmer took lots of punches to the face, and he has a cut under his right eye. His manager and trainers are working on him. It is of note to say that Fullmer has had sixty professional fights and has only been knocked out, once in his career, by the legendary Sugar Ray Robinson. After October, he would have gone five years without a knockout. (*Pause*) A right jab to Fullmer's ear.

(*Cheering*)

ANNOUNCER. Both boxers are working to the body, punching to the body.

(*Cheering*)

ANNOUNCER. Fullmer has boxed three draws in his career in the NBA. The first was with Giardello, the second with Sugar Ray Robinson, and the third with Dick Tiger early this year. (*Bell*) Round four. They tie one another up. Makes one wonder whether this is a wrestling tournament. (*Cheers*) There's Tiger taking those jabs from Fullmer on his gloves. (*Bell*) That's the end of round four. (*Bell*) Round five. A good left to Fullmer's face from Tiger. Another left hook to Fullmer's ears. Fullmer retaliates with a hook to Tiger's. (*Pause*) Again, Tiger beating Fullmer to the punch. Twenty seconds to the end of the fifth round!

(*Chants of "Tiga! Tiga! Tiga!" Chief JMJ, T.O.S. Benson, and Dr. K.O. Mbadiwe circulate the ringside once again, greeting the dignitaries, while the audience in the upper and middle row seats chants their initials.*)

ANNOUNCER. Tiger has gone the full fifteen rounds on three different occasions in his boxing career: the first time was with Will Greaves in 1958; the second time was when he won the middleweight championship from Gene Fullmer in San Francisco, and the third was in Las Vegas, when he fought a draw with Gene Fullmer. Tiger still looks young and fresh, completely unmarked, unfazed! Tiger, of course, has a two-inch advantage over Fullmer in his reach. Two left and rights from Tiger to Fullmer's face. (*Cheers*) Two more good shots to the face by Tiger. They tie one another up. Fullmer's right eye is bleeding now. They tie one another up again. There's bleeding slightly above Fullmer's right eyelid. (*Bell*) End of Round five.

ANNOUNCER. Dick Tiger, the current middleweight champion will be thirty-four next week on Wednesday. Tiger has boxed sixty-two professional fights with twenty-six knockouts and three draws; one was in his last fight with Fullmer in Las Vegas. Fullmer turned thirty-two three weeks ago. He's had sixty professional fights.

ANNOUNCER. There's blood on Fullmer's right eye, but we don't know how bad it is, and they should be able to work on that eye before the next round. We know Fullmer to be a very tough, rugged fighter. (*Bell*) Bleeding of Fullmer's right eye seems to have been stopped. Two good hits on the face and body; the cut on Fullmer's eye is open again. Now Fullmer is bleeding from the nose. Another good left and right from Tiger onto Fullmer's face. (*Cheers. Then the sound of a bell.*) End of round six!

(*Pause*) Jersey Jones, Bobby Diamond, and Jimmy August on Tiger's side. They've been with Tiger since he went over to the USA. (*Astonished*) Oh! Fullmer's manager is waving for the fight to stop! Oh! The fight has been stopped! (*Yelling*) Dick Tiger is declared the winner! (*Loudly*) The whole place is in pandemonium! Dick Tiger has been declared the winner on technical knockout! Jack Hart, the sole judge in this fight, called the first round even and gave the rest to Tiger. The Associated Press, on the other hand, gave all seven rounds to Tiger! Dick Tiger has won on technical knockout at the end of the sixth and start of the seventh round! Gene Fullmer retired with a badly cut eye. So, Dick Tiger is still the world champion!

Goldsmith. After the fight; in a show of gallantry and true sportsmanship, the bruised-up Fullmer walked to the center of the ring and congratulated Tiger, to the delirium of excitement of the crowd.

DICK TIGER SR. Utter pandemonium gripped the stadium, as thirty-five thousand people, intoxicated by the ecstasy of the moment, let out shrill, deafening sounds. A handful of them injected themselves onto the stage to personally congratulate me, screaming, "Tiga, don' kill am! Tiga, don' kill am! Tiga, don' kill am!"

GOLDSMITH. But the hysterical fans were quickly booted off the stage by riot police stationed at the stadium. Even some of the press corps seated at ringside had their typewriters knocked to the ground in the hoopla.

DICK TIGER SR. My victory was finally announced through the public address system about ten minutes after I was declared the winner. The stadium reverberated with cheers and adulations.

Champions Dick Tiger and Gene Fullmer in a duel for the WBA championship belt.

Orisa di n'elu, please give him a heart to love and to be loved.

—Ihetu Ugboaja

GOLDSMITH. Governor-General Dr. Nnamdi Azikiwe issued a statement to Dick Tiger.

NNAMDI AZIKIIWE. Dick Tiger, you have once again established your superiority as a kingpin of the middleweights. Continue to be humble and charitable in your disposition but lead a clean life to enable you to give a worthy account of yourself when occasion demands it.

GOLDSMITH. Dr. Azikiwe also lauded Gene Fullmer for his show of true sportsmanship. Fullmer in turn thanked the governor-general and commended the Nigerian people for their exceptional hospitality.

NNAMDI AZIKIWE. Gene Fullmer, you have done remarkably well. You have impressed Nigerians by your skill and sportsmanship. We are proud to have you as our guest because you are an embodiment of American clean-living and never-say-die attitude. Better luck to you.

GENE FULLMER, *graciously*. I never thought that the Nigerian people would treat me so kindly. You know, they gave me almost as big a hand as Dick got when I entered the ring. I have no regrets. I thought I hit him a few good ones, but he just kept coming. The way Dick Tiger fought tonight, he could have beaten the best of any middleweights I have ever met in the ring.

GOLDSMITH. The match had been over for about thirty minutes when Tiger, growing weary, pleaded for space to be eked out to enable him get to his dressing room. Tiger was visibly moved when hours after the fight, he saw thousands of people waiting outside of his dressing room just to congratulate him. For that one night, the hearts of all Nigerians beat as one. Regardless of ethnicity, tribe, or religion, they all came together as one with one goal: that is Nigeria's promise—Africa's promise—of unity and pride.

Dick Tiger Sr. For weeks after the fight, congratulatory missives poured in from all over the world, including a cabled message from Dr. Kwame Nkrumah, Black Africa's chief proponent of nationalism.

GOLDSMITH. Even the sitting president of the United States of America at the time, President John F. Kennedy himself, also sent his congratulations and goodwill message upon Dick Tiger's triumph in the match in a conversation with Prime Minister Tafawa Balewa on August 23, 1963. Here is an excerpt of their conversation as documented in the American Presidency Project:

THE PRESIDENT. Prime Minister?

PRIME MINISTER BALEWA. Yes.

THE PRESIDENT. It is a great pleasure to talk to you from the White House. We send our very best wishes to your people and to you.

THE PRIME MINISTER. Thank you, Mr. President.

THE PRESIDENT. I hope that this is the beginning of much closer communication between Nigeria and the United States and, indeed, between the whole continent of Africa and our continent, our hemisphere. I think that this can be a very important means of providing for closer understanding among our peoples and also, of course, among the people of Africa.

We send you, particularly, Prime Minister, our best wishes, remembering your visit here to the United States. I also appreciated the wire you sent me in early August in regard to the test ban treaty. I think that what we are doing today shows what can be done through the peaceful use of space.

THE PRIME MINISTER. We congratulate you very heartily, Mr. President, for this very big achievement.

THE PRESIDENT. Prime Minister, I hope we will be seeing you back in the United States and that all goes well for your country and your people.

THE PRIME MINISTER. Thank you.

THE PRESIDENT. Very good wishes, Prime Minister, and we look forward to having Dick Tiger come over here.

THE PRIME MINISTER. It was indeed a very great day for us when Dick Tiger beat the American, Gene Fullmer.

THE PRESIDENT. I know. I know. We watch those things over here. Well, we wish you good luck, Prime Minister, and give our very warmest regards from the people of the United States to the people of Nigeria.

THE PRIME MINISTER. Mr. President, I would be very happy if you would convey our greetings and all the best wishes to the people of the United States.

THE PRESIDENT. Thank you, Prime Minister, and we look forward to seeing you back at the White House again someday.

THE PRIME MINISTER. It is my intention to visit the United States very soon, Mr. President.

THE PRESIDENT. Good. Thank you, Mr. Prime Minister, and goodbye.

Note: The president spoke by telephone at 9:30 a.m. with Prime Minister Sir Abubakar Tafawa Balewa of Nigeria as part of a ceremony formally inaugurating service by the new Syncom II satellite launched July 26. In the course of his remarks, he referred to Dick Tiger of Nigeria, who on August 10 had retained the world middleweight boxing championship by defeating Gene Fullmer of Utah at Ibadan, Nigeria.

Act Thirteen

SCENE ONE

GOLDSMITH. It is now early evening, and with the end of the captivating narration of the civil war experiences, the herculean task of hosting the world championship match and hearing about Dick Tiger's childhood experiences, everyone, though marveled by the events, is spent and ready to retire home, but not before my good friend, Dick Tiger, has to quell a mob attack!

CHINAKA, *amazed*. Ewooh! Diki my broda, you are great for the country! All these things happen in the country because of you! *(Proudly)* Even number one person in America call to say congratulate to Nigerians. Is really great!

GOLDSMITH, *excitedly*. Wow! President John F. Kennedy himself is congratulating us. *(Amazed)* Wow! Other congratulatory messages came too from outside of the African countries. *(Raising his fists.)* Congratulations to you, Diki! *(Pause)* Now I understand why they say you, put Nigeria on the map!

CHORUS, *standing*. Nzogbu! Nzogbu! Enyimba! Enyi! Nzogbu! Enyimba! *(Chanted twice)*

NELSON. Nwanne'm nwoke, (my brother,) you do great! *(Fighting back tears.)* When I think of where we come from the back village, to pickin' bottles in streets, and to your many many world champion boxings, (*raising both hands to the sky*) I jus say, "Orisa, thank you!"

GODWIN, *elated.* Eyiooh! You are really a great broda! You be a great son of the soil. Look how all the peoples, oyibos from all over world come to our country to watch you, Taatu son, fight *(Quickly)* and win in front the hole wold! *(Shrieks)* Ennyii mmbba!

DICK TIGER SR. *smiling warmly.* It was indeed a defining moment in our country when we hosted the world championship. Everyone, even our politicians, witnessed firsthand the great merits of a united front.

NELSON. If you think back, (*pauses*) all this celebration with the country happened only seven years ago. *(Frowning)* And now they is war already? I don't think they thinking right.

GOLDSMITH. If only our leaders will hearken to what binds us as a nation, and not let any groups become like the unruly child—

GODWIN, *confused.* What child you dey talk?

GOLDSMITH, *seriously.* No, I am not talking about any child but just saying that if groups of people are treated right in the country, in respect of their civil rights, they will not want to leave, you know, like the Igbos, for example. (*Pause*) We don't want to become like the unruly child, always seeking a divorce from his abusive parents, but the more he protests the abuse they give him, the harsher the degree of punishment inflicted upon him.

DICK TIGER SR, *wearily.* No, that will not make for peace.

GOLDSMITH. Exactly, Diki. One doesn't have to be a psychologist or fortune- teller to forecast a disastrous outcome for such a relationship. Rather, when the parents sit with the child to identify his problem, and help him to feel wanted and loved, then there will be peace, and that child will not want a divorce from his parents. He will be deferential to his parents and would happily work with them to build their home.

NELSON, *looking confused.* Ewooh! Gordy Goldsmith, you and this divorce of a thin' is making me scare. *(They laugh.)* Are you divorce your wi—

(They are startled by shrieks of "Onye oshi! (Thief!) Onye oshi!" (Thief!) and "Kill am! Kill am!" followed by quick, heavy stomping coming up the stairs and terrified screams of children running up same stairs, in front of a chubby, disheveled middle-aged man. A maid, hearing the commotion, comes upon the scene and quickly slams the door shut, but just as the strange man bolts inside. A sea of people had already taken up all space down below the inside of the square-shaped veranda; each, in one hand clutching their wares on their heads, and the other carrying a stick or a baseball- sized stone.)

MAID, *forcefully.* Stop right there!

(The man staggers, bleeding from a gash on his head that makes a trail of blood from the stairwell to the corner of the veranda, where all out of breath, he heaves himself smack on the concrete floor, just as Abigail, Dick Tiger, and his guests rush to the scene. Tiger's house robe is slightly undone exposing his bandaged ribcage; and he strains to walk with his shoulders bent. As the crowd sights Tiger, they grow silent. He did not have to say or do much to assuage the crowd. A maid bolts to get a bucket of water to mop up the bloodied veranda and stairwell.)

DICK TIGER SR, *struggles to raise both hands, and speaks with a strained, but high-pitched tone.* Umu Aba oma, (Beautiful people of Aba,) I greet you all! *(As if programmed, one by one, each person in the crowd drops whatever object they are carrying, to inflict pain upon said "Onye oshi". They start clapping. After about two minutes, Tiger tries again to put his hands up to motion them to cease clapping. They stop, and he continues.)*

If this man *(Pointing at the man on the ground.)* has annoyed you in any way, I ask you in the name of God Almighty to forgive him. We will make sure that he pays for whatever wrong he has done. *(As he speaks, some in the crowd stretch their necks, giraffe-like, to get a glance at the champion, and some gently place their wares on the ground to be able to get a good look at him.)*

I know we are all feeling a lot of pressure nowadays to just survive. Don't give up on life. Don't give in to despair. *(Pauses)* Remember my story. *(Pauses)* You can still thrive. Just keep working hard, and trusting in the grace of God. *(Pauses)* Be good to one another. *(Pauses)* I will get the police to come and take him away. He will go before a judge, and when found guilty, he will be punished for his crime. *(Pauses)* Take up your wares, and go fetch food for yourselves and your families.

(Waving to them.) Bye-bye.

(As quickly as they came, one by one they filed out onto the streets without a word, back to their daily hustle and bustle.)

CHINAKA, *whispering.* Diki, God bless you! You save am.

DICK TIGER SR, *calling to his assistant.* Ebere! Where are you? *(Deepens voice)* You know, maybe the man doesn't know how to cope in these austere times like we all are coping, or he may well be innocent, *(mumbles)* but we will soon get the facts.

GOLDSMITH. Well, he should just thank his lucky stars that you were on hand to save his life. *(Ebere appears)*

EBERE. Yes, Sir.

DICK TIGER SR. Quickly, contact the Deputy Superintendent of Police, (DSP) Ubani. Ask him to come and arrest this man.

EBERE. Yes, Sir. Right away, Sir. *(He bolts.)*

DICK TIGER SR, *Tiger's kids, Justina, Charles, Richard, and Victoria run towards him and give him gentle hugs.* You were scared? There is nothing to be afraid of. Just be cautious when you are playing outside. Don't be afraid. Okay?

CHORUS. Yes, Papa.

DICK TIGER SR, *looking intently into their eyes.* Don't be afraid. *(Kisses each child on the forehead.)* Be strong. May God bless you, my children.

JUSTINA. Thank you, Papa. *(They leave.)*

Champion Dick Tiger's last portrait with his children. Circa 1971.

GOLDSMITH, *scratching his head.* Today has truly proved unforgettable!

NELSON AND GODWIN. Yes O!

GODWIN. For sure. (*Counting off his fingers*) We talk about big boxing, the war, and we see Diki save a life, again! All in one day.

CHINAKA. You mean, save one more life. (Pauses) He save another life to add to the thousands he save during the Biafra war. Truth. Them crowds want kill that man. Some of them even carry old tire to use burn him alife! I wonda wetin him steal.

GODWIN. Even if na only one orange wey him steal, they go wan kill am (*Pause*) hungar dey too much now for country. (*Pauses*) That man for just die for nothin' if Diki no come save am. Diki, big broda, thank you. May Orisa bless you.

DICK TIGER SR., *wearily.* My gentlemen, brothers, it's been a blast! Thank you so much for all the great memories. May God bless you all.

CHORUS. Amen!

CHINAKA. God bless you, Diki. (*Pause*) I will travel back to the village in about a week time, but I go come see you again before leaving.

GOLDSMITH. Diki, thank you very much for everything, brother! I will be traveling to the village for a few days as well, and will come check on you once I return to Aba.

DICK TIGER SR. Goodbye all. Thank you.

Scene Two

GOLDSMITH. Less than a week since going down memory lane with his bosom buddies, around mid-afternoon on a sunny, breezy harmattan day in December, Dick Tiger, my best friend, breathed his last. The skies were a hue of powder blue. Piercing cries of seagulls that occasionally roam Aba skies seemed to sound the death knell, more temperamental and chaotic, striking as if to foreshadow death. The serenity of the harmattan afternoon was disrupted by wails, the deep, gutsy kind that signifies deep loss and sorrow, coming from the upper chamber in Dick Tiger's room. The great iroko tree has been felled. How are the mighty fallen? Dick Tiger, the African warrior and hero, passed on to his ancestors in the great beyond. Arrangements were urgently made to contact his siblings and extended family members. Arrangements were made assiduously to conduct his funeral.

MAID, *shrieking.* Deadoh! Deadoh! Oh! Oh! *(Concerned neighbors gather and try to console her. Incoherently, she points towards a room as Abigail emerges.)*

ABIGAIL, *distraught, destabilized, she storms out of the room, gnashing her teeth and hitting her head hard on the hard wall. People rush in to restrain her.* Diki! *(Raising both hands, sobbing.)* God help me! Help! Help! Help me! *(Rambling)* Papa umu'm! (My children's father!) *(Shrieking)* Oh! Death! *(Mumbles)* Wicked! Death! Wicked!

GOLDSMITH. Abigail is quickly restrained and a doctor is called in to assess her condition. Tiger's residence was now swarming with mourners; people stricken by the news of Tiger's demise. Abigail is promptly sedated when Dr. Nzeribe called, and Dick Tiger's body is taken to St. Anthony's Hospital for official pronouncements.

(GODWIN and NELSON and CHINAKA *arrive, faces wet with tears.*)

CHINAKA, *slowly and sadly, one hand over his chest.* Diki, my great broda, you will be always remembered for good. *(Sobbing)*

NELSON, *lost in the teaming crowds gathering, appraises the scenario for a minute, then turns his tear-drenched face quickly from the crowd and weeps uncontrollably.* Death, onye oshi! Robbery! Heartbreaker! life spoiler! Ewooh! My dear broda, Diki, may God continue to bless you, and give you life in death. Amin. *(He stands in the middle of the crowd, his mind wracked with despair. He feels hopeless but picks himself up to deal with the crushing blow death has dealt them. He resolves to do right by his amiable brother, Diki.)*

GODWIN, *runs far away from Tiger's premises to find a place to cry, but there were teams of mourners wherever he turned. He runs into a fenced garden, and there in the protection of the walled garden lets the tears roll, drenching his shirt so much so it clung to his body, as if in fear.* Rest in peace, nwanne'm oma. Diki tiga, wold champion, God will give you rest. *(Pauses)* Amin.

(The brothers meet, pull themselves together in order to ensure that their famous brother, Dick Tiger, gets a burial that befits his name and legacy.)

Chinaka Ihetu

Nelson

Godwin in his youth

Gordy "Goldsmith" Uzoaru

DICK TIGER

Afterword

In less than a year after Dick Tiger announced his retirement from boxing, he lost the fight with a different, deadlier kind of opponent—cancer. Few months before his passing, he had applied for a return of his passport that had been seized by the Federal Immigration Service upon his return. He needed to travel to America at the request of his doctors to undergo a radical, experimental course of treatment for cancer. His request was denied, citing his involvement in the Biafra war. Dick Tiger—the enigma in boxing, the African battler—succumbed to liver cancer at the onset of middle age. He breathed his last on December 14, 1971. He was only forty-two years old.

His body was laid in state for days at his residence in Aba. Throngs of mourners lined up daily to be able to get a last glimpse and pay him their last respects. With the news of his demise, condolences and eulogies poured in from around the world—all of which attested to the high regard he was held in, both as a man and a fighter. On the following Sunday after his death, his body was taken to his village of Amaigbo in an entourage comprising a number of government officials from the East Central and Midwestern States, sports aficionados, and a few federal government officials who came on their own account. In Amaigbo, the scene was no different as crowds of people swarmed the Holy Trinity Anglican church, where the funeral service was presided over by the Reverend John Kirkpatrick. Afterwards, Dick Tiger was committed to his place of rest, in his estate, in Amaigbo. He was accorded the premium honor of a twenty-one-gun salute.

The day was rounded up with various activities, including boxing exhibitions. He was survived by his wife Abigail, eight children, his aged mother, and three brothers.

Dame Abigail carried the torch for her late husband superfluously. As matriarch of the Ihetu clan, she was rooted in the promises of the word of God as her source of strength and refuge. Widowed at only thirty-six years old with eight young children, she relied on her spiritual foundation in the task of raising her children and maintaining a synergy with the rest of the ever-growing Ihetu clan. She passed on in October 2008 at the age of seventy-three. The children she raised, now middle-aged men and women holding their own in their chosen fields, continue to cherish her memory.

While Dick Tiger's death was premature, his life was indeed a tale of progress and self-improvement: from humble beginnings to a wealthy realtor; from street fighter in obscure boxing booths to global recognition and acclaim. I hope the young people who read this book will dare to have big dreams as well. Despite the peaks and valleys in Dick Tiger's career and life, he remained undaunted. His career record was a total of eighty-one bouts: sixty-one victories and seventeen losses, with three draws, and twenty-six knockouts.

Tiger was a man of many talents, but above all, he was a humanitarian. Though he promoted peace, he stood against social injustice. His activism drew him to fight in the Biafra war, in protest of the pogroms directed at the Igbos, and some argue that his reputation as a heroic figure has been overshadowed by his involvement in Nigeria's civil war. During the war, he was a symbol of strength, hope, and affirmation for the Biafrans. He wanted to make things right for them in the face of the pervading injustice that they faced in their homeland. He used his money, time, and status as a world champion boxer to disseminate news of the atrocities of the war globally, in order to evoke sympathy and garner support for the Biafran's cause of a secession from the Nigerian Republic.

Dick Tiger never cut corners and loathed mediocrity, always attending to his career and life with dexterity and devotion. This explains why during the Biafra war he did not sit on the sidelines but approached the catastrophe of the war head on. He was enraged by the atrocities of the war: the bombings, killings, the politically engineered hunger and starvation of the Biafrans. Exacerbated by the carnage, he gave all he could to assuage the mayhem. He gave up his personal cars, including his treasured Mercedes Benz, to assist in carting the injured to the hospital and in delivering dead bodies to the morgues for proper burial. On the boxing stage, he insisted on being introduced as, Dick Tiger of Biafra! He famously accused the British of siding with the Nigerian Federal Forces in the daily killings and bombings of the Igbos by their hundreds, and to drive his point home, he willingly returned the coveted MBE Civil Medal awarded him by Queen Elizabeth II back to the British Embassy in Washington, D.C.

It is difficult to reconcile Dick Tiger's deep devotion to his people with the lack luster support that has been meted to him since his demise and by the same people for whom he sacrificed his illustrious career and ultimately, his life. Dick Tiger's reputation as a beacon of hope and a source of inspiration for his people is lost on a whole generation of his countrymen as a result of the collective amnesia and selfishness of some of those same people, he "walked on fire" for. It goes without saying that Dick Tiger has been treated shabbily by the deafening silence of those for whom he sacrificed so much. But posterity will always remember him with reverence and appreciation, for his contributions to humanity.

After the civil war, he lost most of his business holdings, and his properties were confiscated by the federal government. His home state seized his school, which he had completed at the height of the civil war, in his hometown of Amaigbo. However, decades since Tiger's passing, his erstwhile battered image has been experiencing a gradual but steady resuscitation. His properties had since been returned to his family, with the exception of his school, the Dick Tiger Memorial Secondary School (DTMSS). That notwithstanding, his family has not forfeited the right to petition and remains steadfast on a reconciliatory return of said school to its rightful owners.

DickTiger continues to garner international and national awards and accolades decades after his demise. Some say that his legacy is like an eternal flame—the kind that either shines or burns through.

It is reported that after the civil war, the "Article of Surrender" was signed by the chief architects of the war on the Biafra side, which proclaimed, "No Victors, No Vanquished." The Snr. secessionist officers led by Major General Phillip Asuquo Effiong, gave up secession and accepted the spirit of one Nigeria. They affirmed and pledged their allegiance to the Federal Republic of Nigeria. The Article was purported to be a show of intent by the federal forces—the "victors"—to begin the healing process in the country and reintegrate the "vanquished." Dick Tiger died believing, like the rest of the survivors at the time, in the integrity of said proclamation. He had shared, with family, friends and acquaintances, his hopes for Nigeria's future with the war's end. In his very last fight, in July, 1970, when asked about his future plans, Tiger replied, "About the war in my country, I am glad that we are one again. I will go back to my country in a few months to see my people." He had high hopes, as did the other survivors of the war, that the discord and injustice—causal effects of the war—had been defeated with the end of the civil war. He believed that post-civil war, his country would acquire the strength of spirit as well as the sense of purpose to plod on in harmony as one nation, to claim their rightful place in the world's sphere. He died holding on to the hope of a harmonious and more vibrant homeland, even greater than the one which a few years earlier had hosted a world championship—the very first of its kind on African soil. Unfortunately, more than fifty years since that signage, said proclamation continues to ring hallow. The civil war was not only a defining moment for Nigeria but has regrettably continued to define the country decades later. The debate about the viability of Nigeria's union rages on, and the jury is still out on the verdict.

Almost fifty-three years after the civil war, it is believed that policies instituted by Nigeria's Federal Government have emboldened and enlarged the scope of the "vanquished" as many more states join in the clamor for justice and fairness. For a few years now, indigenous groups, like an engine habitually pushed beyond the red line, have backed up and abruptly shut down their belief in the realism or realization of one Nigeria. They feel dispossessed and have been organizing peaceful protests and rallies across the country demanding self-actualization. Dick Tiger and all of the other faithfully departed patriots must be turning in their graves. They would be wondering, "How could this be?" It looks like history repeating itself. But it would be foolhardy and a fairytale to believe that there will soon be the likes of the champion, Dick Tiger, to come like a knight in shining armor, bearing unbridled sacrifices to benefit throngs of his down trodden fellow countrymen from the atrocities and calamities of war.

Nigeria cannot afford another war as the country is still reeling from the residuals of the civil war. The plight suffered by the Nigerian state during the civil war should serve as a basis of inspiration to all Nigerians to strive for peace, unity, and justice, for all.

The civil war in Nigeria and the struggles to rebuild continues to impact all Nigerians. It has proved painful to revisit and write about the Nigerian civil war atrocities, death and killings, that Dick Tiger lamented so much about. But I write. Because it is imperative that each new generation of Nigerians know what happened in Nigeria's fledgling democracy with the abdication of power by the British colonists. It is the patriotic duty of every citizen of the country to ensure that generations do not forget their shared past and values. My hope is that this knowledge would cause them to be vigilant; and safeguard the freedom and peace that can be snatched away so abruptly.

Some of the greatest statesmen, including notable historians and psychologists, have cautioned nations and leaders against neglecting history. They urge countries and their peoples to study history, so that the secrets of statecraft may be revealed to prevent the catastrophe that results from repeating the errors of the past.

In our history are comprised the lens through which we can reflect and evaluate our checkered past. Through this lens we can move our country forward, to be what we want it to be - strong, united, progressive. To date, there is no official history of the Nigerian Civil War. None, not even from the "vanquished."

When history is shunned, generations are deprived the opportunity to actively explore and bring their own critical scrutiny to events in the country's historical documents, to find out for themselves the essence of their country's history, and to help them chart their hopes for her future.

I needed to give a sense of continuity and knowledge of Nigeria's remarkable history. I began by writing, In Africa's Honor, Dick Tiger Versus Gene Fullmer III: A Blast from Nigeria's Glorious Past, which documents Nigeria's convulsive race to bring the world boxing championship to the shores of Africa. Nigerians were at their best; as they banded together to achieve the herculean task of hosting a world championship fight, the first of its kind in Africa, sans apartheid South Africa.

The Nigerian nation is replete with glorious and inglorious pasts too much for us to continue to pretend that history is irrelevant. It is our hope and prayer that our leaders will embrace a sense of history and focus on only what binds Nigerians together as a people.

Sir Alhaji Abubakar Tafawa Balewa, who later became Nigeria's first prime minister, spoke about Nigeria's unique character in his speech marking the nation's march towards independence in 1957. He stressed that Nigeria's greatness as a country is dependent on the unity of the country. He continues:

> "Indeed, unity today is our greatest concern, and it is the duty of every one of us to work so that we may strengthen it. The peoples of Nigeria must be united to enable this country to play a full part in shaping the destiny of mankind. On no account should we allow the selfish ambitions of individuals to jeopardize the peace of the thirty-three million law-abiding people of Nigeria. It is the duty of all

of us to work for unity and encourage members
of all our communities to live together in peace
and harmony."

Barely ten years after this auspicious speech by Sir Tafawa
Balewa, the fledgling Nigerian nation had been marred by coups
and countercoups. At last count, Nigeria recorded over two hundred
million people strong, but recent events indicate that Nigerians
have overlooked the struggles of the founding fathers as a passing
phase in some distant past, and for that, her citizenry continue
to pay the price. We have neglected to heed to the wise caution
etched in the words of Nigeria's founding fathers and for that, the
whirlwinds of revolt continue to rattle and shake the foundations
of the Nigerian Federation today, decades after Nigeria gained
independence.

Most of the citizenry of Nigeria truly desire to live peaceably
and in harmony irrespective of ethnic, cultural and religious
differences, but not at the expense of their inalienable rights as
citizens of the country. Nigeria's union they contend, is jeopardized
when the judiciary and other arms of government are compromised.
Unity, peace and harmony they maintain, should come effortlessly,
with freedom; devoid of any form of dictation.

Standing on the shoulders of my late father, the great Dick
Tiger and the millions of people whose lives were cut short in
the struggle for their civil rights, I say that it is time to draw the
curtain on the war and rampage against the vast number of hapless
Nigerians who continue to feel neglected and deprived of their
inalienable rights in the affairs of governance. It is a daily prayer of
most Nigerians that the leadership of Nigeria will shun bias and
prejudice, but continue to devise ways to keep Nigeria's diversity
vibrant in tackling the challenges of governance today.

My hope, and I dare say, the hope of many Nigerians, is that
Nigeria's children will learn to see themselves not in the usual
stereotypic way, but as part of a shared heritage. As my father's
daughter I know that it is important for us to cherish our own

special heritage, but above everything else, we must be able to celebrate our humanity.

Nigeria's failure as a country will be possible only if her people should ignore the history of Nigeria's struggles as a nation. Nigerians owe it to themselves to identify and embrace their shared core values, their rich heritage—the multiplicity of ethnicities and cultures that is Nigeria's union. A united Nigeria is possible only when Nigerians remain undaunted in their resolve to honor the ideals of nationhood and patriotism for which their Founding Fathers fought.

Accolades and Accomplishments of Dick Tiger

1. Nigerian Middleweight Champion, 1955
2. British common wealth champion, March 27, 1958
3. Member of the Civil Division of the Most Excellent Order of the British Empire (MBE) by Queen Elizabeth II of Great Britain.
4. World Middleweight Boxing Champion, October 23, 1962
5. The Edward J. Neill Trophy Memorial for Outstanding Service to Boxing in 1963 and 1966. By Boxing Writers' Association of New York.
6. Sport Lodge BiNai Brith Twelfth Annual Award in 1963 for high principles and achievement in sports.
7. Norwich Union Trophy for Nigerian Sportsman of the Year, 1961, 1962, 1963, 1965, and 1966.
8. World Light Heavyweight Boxing Champion, Dec 16,1966
9. Gentleman Jim Award, Schaefer Circle of Sports, October 18,1968
10. Rated the 50th Best Boxer of All Time dating back 1880. The first and only African so named.
11. 31st best Boxer in the last 80 years. The first and only African so-named.

12. The only boxer to win Ring Magazine Fighter of the Year Award twice, in the 1960's. He won this distinguished award in 1962 and 1965.
13. Single-handedly built a secondary school in an underserved rural community.
14. Elected to the Ring Magazine Hall of Fame, (BHF) in 1974
15. Elected to the Nigerian Boxing Hall of Fame (BHF) in 1987
16. Elected to the World Boxing Hall of Fame (BHF) in 1987
17. Elected to the International Boxing Hall of Fame, in 1991
18. National Honors conferred by H.E. President Good Luck Jonathan's regime in 2014.
19. Elected to the New York State Boxing Hall of Fame in 2016.
20. State Honors conferred by H.E Rochas Okorocha in 2018.

Timeline

August 14, 1929: Dick Tiger was born Richard Ihetu in the village of Amaigbo, in the Eastern Region of the British Protectorate of Nigeria.

October 1943: Left for Enugu, capital of the Eastern Region.

January 1944: Left for Aba Township. Began bottle recycling with his brothers, Nelson and Godwin.

March 1949: Tiger began boxing in the amateur division.

September 1952: Tiger had his first professional bout. A spike in the levy assessed for entertainment events lead to a recession in the boxing industry.

December 1952: Tiger lost to Tommy West in Aba but afterwards was invited to fight at the Collister Belt Tournament.

January 1953: Decisions Blackie Power, the Nigerian middleweight champion in a non-title contest.

May 1953: Lost in the seventh round of a middleweight title contest with Tommy West.

January 1954: Lost to Tommy West for the third time.

October 1955: Tiger sailed for Liverpool to be managed by Peter Banasko.

December 1955: Tiger's first fight in Britain ended in a points loss to Alan Dean. Suffered three more agonizing losses in a row.

March 1957: Tiger joined Liverpool manager Tony Vairo's stable of fighters.

February 1958: Married Abigail Ogbuji, and later brought her to London, England.

March 1958: Tiger won the British Empire middleweight title by knocking out Patrick McAteer at Liverpool Stadium.

May 1957: TKO's Terry Downes in seven rounds, Shoreditch Town Hall, London.

June 1958: Lost British Empire middleweight crown to Ellsworth "Spider" Webb.

June 1959: Made his American debut by drawing with Rory Calhoun at New York's Madison Square Garden.

October 1, 1960: Nigeria gained her independence from Britain.

November, 1960: Won back the British Commonwealth middleweight title from Canada's Wilf Greaves in Edmonton Canada.

October 23,1962: Tiger defeated Gene Fullmer to win the N.B.A, world middleweight title.

February 1963: Retained his middleweight crown by drawing with Gene Fullmer.

July 1963: Awarded the M.B.E. medal of the British distinguished list by Her Excellency Queen Elizabeth II.

August 10, 1963: Knocked out Gene Fullmer in Ibadan, Nigeria. The fight is the first world title fight to be staged in Black Africa.

December 1963: Lost his title to Joey Giardello in Atlantic City's first world boxing championship.

September 1964: His bout with Don Fullmer at the Cleveland Arena is Madison Square Garden's last of the weekly televised fights run for twenty years in partnership with the Gillette Corporation.

October 1965: After two torturous years regained his middleweight boxing championship from Giardello, making him the oldest world champion still in the fight game.

January 1966: An army mutiny orchestrated by mostly Igbo officers from Dick Tiger's ethnic group brought the first Republic to an end.

April, 1966: Tiger suffered a controversial loss of his middle weight title to Emile Griffith.

May 1966: Pogroms ensue, directed mainly at the Igbo community in Northern Nigeria.

July 1966: A second mutiny, this time effected by officers of Northern origin overthrew the military government. Ironsi; many soldiers of Igbo origin are slain.

August 1966: Lt. Colonel Gowon took the reins as the supreme military figure, after Maj. General Ironsi's execution.

October 1966: Igbo communities in Northern Nigeria were subjected to further pogroms.

December 1966: At Madison Square Garden Tiger defeated Jose Torres to become only the second fighter in sixty-three years to win the world light heavyweight title in addition to middleweight class.

February 1967: Boxed in a non-title bout in Port Harcourt city to raise money for Eastern refugees fleeing the North and other parts of Nigeria.

May 1967: Tiger retained his title against Jose Torres.

June 1967: Dick Tiger publicly declared his allegiance to the Biafran state and renounced all associations with Nigeria.

July 1967: The civil war officially began in Nigeria.

December 1967: Tiger received a commission as a second lieutenant in the Biafran Army Morale Corps.

May 1968: Lost his world light heavyweight title to Bob Foster; the only time he was knocked out in his career.

October 1968: Subdued Frankie Depaula in a non-title bout to merit Ring Magazine's "Fight of the Year" ranking.

December 1969: Returns his M.B.E. medal to the British Embassy in Washington D.C.

January 1970: Biafra surrendered, ending the thirty-month long Nigerian Civil War.

July 1970: Lost to Emile Griffith in what turned out to be his final professional bout.

July 1971: Announced his retirement from boxing, and applied for a guarantee of safe passage into Nigeria at the Nigerian Embassy in New York.

He is guaranteed safe passage by the Nigerian government, and he left the shores of America back to his homeland of Nigeria.

October 1971: While in Nigeria, he requested for a return of his travel documents seized by NIS upon his entry into Nigeria but was denied.

December 14, 1971: Died of complications from liver cancer, in Aba, and is buried in his hometown of Amaigbo.

Resources

Books

Coleman, S. James. Nigeria: *Background to Nationalism*. University of California Press, 1958.

Downes, Terry. *My Bleedin' Business—An Autobiography*. Sun Lakes: Robson Books, 1989.

Ifaturoti, Damola. *Dick Tiger—The Life and Times of Africa's Most Accomplished World Boxing Champion*. Princeton: Sungai Books, 2002

Makinde, Ade. *Dick Tiger—The Life and Times of a Boxing Immortal*. Tarentum: Word Association Publishers, 2004.

Newspapers, Journals, and Magazines

Garrison, Lloyd. "Details Settled on Tiger-Fullmer Fight" The New York Times. May 23, 1963.

Garrison, Lloyd. "Nigerians Afraid Fullmer's Afraid" The New York Times July 6, 1963.

Garrison, Lloyd. "Fullmer's Bid for New Delay Has Dick Tiger Burning Bright" The New York Times. July 13, 1963.

Garrison, Lloyd. "Fight is One-Sided" The New York Times, August 11, 1963

Garrison, Lloyd. "Fullmer Heads Home" The New York Times, August 12, 1963.

Goodman, Murray. "I'll Try Again" The Ring, March 15, 1963.

Ihetu, Dick Tiger. "The Fight of My Life." The Ring, October 24, 1962.

Johnson, Charles. "Nigeria's One and Only Tiger" Institute of Current World Affairs (ICWA) July 22, 1963.

Liosa, Luis Fernando. "Gene Fullmer, Boxer" SI Vault, January 19, 2004.

McCloud, Roderick. "No Victor, No Vanquished: Remembering Biafra". July 6, 2017.

Mooney, John. "A Juju Side Bet". Salt Lake Tribune. April 27, 1963.

Neold, Dennis. "Nigerian Hires Rain Man to Protect Title Battle" The Robesonian Sports August 6, 1963.

Olson, Jack. "A Smile on the Face of a Tiger". SI Vault, August 19, 1963.

Onumah, Chido. "Of Victors and Vanquished: Biafra 50 Years After" The Cable, January 10, 2020

Rogin, Gilbert. "The Tattooed Tiger from Nigeria". SI Vault, November 5, 1962.

Zukas, Lorna Lueker. "Women's War of 1929". IEO, August 14, 2008.

"Crocodile on Tiger's Side for Title Fight", Waterloo Daily Courier (Waterloo). August 9, 1963

"Despite Delay, Tiger Heads For Nigeria", Oakland Tribune, June 24, 1963.

"Dick Tiger and Fullmer Fight in San Fran." Milwaukee Sentinel, October 13, 1962.

"Dick Tiger Keeps Title as Fullmer is Unable to Continue Fight After 7th" Special to The New York Times, August 11, 1963.

"Dick Tiger to Face Gene Fullmer in Title Bout" Appleton Post Crescent March 31, 1963.

"Fight Promoter Visits Nigeria" The Billings Gazette. March 29, 1963.

"Fullmer's Foot Halts Next Bout" The High Pointe Enterprise. July 12, 1963

"Fullmer Says He Feels Great" Daily Herald. August 8, 1963.

"Fullmer's Manager Calls Conference" Daily Times Nigeria. August 6, 1963

"Middleweight Bout Set For Saturday" The Morning Herald. August 4, 1963.

"Nigerian Called 'Fighter of the Year'" The New York Times. October 23, 1962.

"Nigerian Government Upset Over Bout" The Post (Frederick, Md.) July 13, 1963.

"Nigeria Gives Gene Fullmer Top Billing" Daily Northwestern. August 2, 1963.

"Nigeria Ready For Big Show." Section 3, Page 5. Wisconsin State Journal. August 9, 1963.

"Nigerians Roar Support for Their Champ" The Fresno Bee. August 10, 1963.

"Nigeria Underwrites Tiger-Fullmer Match" The Portsmouth Times (Portsmouth, OH). August 9, 1963.

"Tiger-Fullmer Fight Reset For August 10" The News (Frederick, Md.) July 12, 1963.

"Title Fight Still On, Promoter Says" Daily Herald. July 11, 1963

"Tiger Retains His Middleweight Title" The Pharos Tribune and Logansport Press, Indiana. August 11, 1963.

"Tiger Risks Title Today", The Post Standard. August 10, 1963

"Tiger TKO's Fullmer." Associated Press, August 10, 1963

"Political In-Fighting, Nigerian Challenge." Pacific Stars & Stripes, August 12, 1963

Internet Resources

Peters, Gerhard, and John T. Woolley. "John F. Kennedy, Conversation with the Prime Minister of Nigeria by Means of the Syncom Communications Satellite," *The American Presidency Project* (August 23, 1963): http://www.presidency.ucsb.edu/ws/?pid=9378.

African Examiner
africanexaminer.com/abariot-0712

Black Past
www.blackpast.org/?q=gah/aba-womens-riots
    novemberdecember-1929.

Dick Tiger Foundation
www.dicktigerfoundation.org

Eastside Boxing
www.eastsideboxing.com/news.php?p=18564&more-1

Encyclopedia.com   www.revolutionprotestencyclopedia.com/.../
    media/IEO Women's _War_of_1929

Historians.org
www.historians.org

Nigeria Exchange - Nigeria>History
 www.ngex.com/nigeria/history/aba_womens_riot-htm

Nigeria World
www.nigeriaworld.com/columnistoyeyemi080502html

Wikipedia the free encyclopedia
en.wikipedia.org/wiki/Aba Women's Riot.

Glossary

Aburi Accord: Also called, the Aburi Declaration, is the term used for the agreement reached between the Federal Government of Nigeria's Supreme Military Council and the leadership of the Eastern Region, in Aburi, Ghana, on the 4th and 5th of January, 1967. The meeting was billed as a last-ditch effort to prevent the impending breakout of war in Nigeria following the second military coup and the upheaval that preceded it.

Agbada: African garb generally worn by men, over a pair of matching trousers.

Black Bomber: A reference to the famous American boxer, Joe Louis, nicknamed, the Black Bomber.

Compound: A number of houses, (usually in a village setting) clustered together; each owned and inhabited by an adult male member of the family or clan and his immediate or nuclear family.

Fufu: A type of dough from any of a variety of flour mixes, e.g., cassava, rice, corn, wheat, banana, or yam flour. It is eaten with a hearty type of traditional soup; principally in most of the East and West African countries.

Kwashiorkor: A condition caused by protein deficiency in the diet. Children in poverty-stricken environs are susceptible to suffering from this ailment. Some signs of kwashiorkor include: edema, or swollen face, hands and feet, and bulging stomach caused by fluid retention in the body of the affected child.

Indirect rule: The British used this system of governance to control parts of their colonial empires, particularly in the southeastern parts of Nigeria.

Nze: A coveted chieftaincy title in southeastern Nigeria conferred on Igbo men who have proven themselves deserving of the title.

Warrant Chiefs: were created by the British colonial government to fill the leadership positions in the south east regions of Nigeria, because the Igbos and Ibibios had no chiefs, but had an egalitarian system of government which recognized authority as coming directly from the people. These warrant chiefs were sadistic, and fabulously corrupt.